Apartheid in South Africa

Apartheid in South Africa

Other titles in the World History series

The Age of Colonialism
Ancient Greece
The Byzantine Empire
The Early Middle Ages
Elizabethan England
The Late Middle Ages
The Nuremberg Trials
The Relocation of the North American Indian
The Roman Empire
The Roman Republic

Apartheid in South Africa

Michael J. Martin

LUCENT BOOKS
A part of Gale, Cengage Learning

Detroit • New York • San Francisco • New Haven, Conn • Waterville, Maine • London

For more information, contact
Lucent Books
27500 Drake Rd.
Farmington Hills, MI 48331-3535
Or you can visit our Internet site at gale.cengage.com

LIBRARY OF CONGRESS CATALOGING-IN-PUBLICATION DATA

Martin, Michael J., 1948-
Apartheid in South Africa / by Michael J. Martin.
p. cm. — (World history series)
Includes bibliographical references and index.
ISBN 1-59018-696-6 (hard cover : alk. paper) 1. Apartheid—South Africa—History—Juvenile literature. 2. Anti-apartheid movements—South Africa—History—Juvenile literature. 3. South Africa—Race relations—History—Juvenile literature. I. Title. II. Series.
DT1757.M375 2006
323.16809—dc22

2005029260

Printed in the United States of America
3 4 5 6 7 12 11 10 09 08

Contents

Foreword

Each year, on the first day of school, nearly every history teacher faces the task of explaining why his or her students should study history. Many reasons have been given. One is that lessons exist in the past from which contemporary society can benefit and learn. Another is that exploration of the past allows us to see the origins of our customs, ideas, and institutions. Concepts such as democracy, ethnic conflict, or even things as trivial as fashion or mores, have historical roots.

Reasons such as these impress few students, however. If anything, these explanations seem remote and dull to young minds. Yet history is anything but dull. And therein lies what is perhaps the most compelling reason for studying history: History is filled with great stories. The classic themes of literature and drama—love and sacrifice, hatred and revenge, injustice and betrayal, adversity and overcoming adversity—fill the pages of history books, feeding the imagination as well as any of the great works of fiction do.

The story of the Children's Crusade, for example, is one of the most tragic in history. In 1212 Crusader fever hit Europe. A call went out from the pope that all good Christians should journey to Jerusalem to drive out the hated Muslims and return the city to Christian control. Heeding the call, thousands of children made the journey. Parents bravely allowed many children to go, and entire communities were inspired by the faith of these small Crusaders. Unfortunately, many boarded ships captained by slave traders, who enthusiastically sold the children into slavery as soon as they arrived at their destination. Thousands died from disease, exposure, and starvation on the long march across Europe to the Mediterranean Sea. Others perished at sea.

Another story, from a modern and more familiar place, offers a soul-wrenching view of personal humiliation but also the ability to rise above it. Hatsuye Egami was one of 110,000 Japanese Americans sent to internment camps during World War II. "Since yesterday we Japanese have ceased to be human beings," he wrote in his diary. "We are numbers. We are no longer Egamis, but the number 23324. A tag with that number is on every trunk, suitcase and bag. Tags, also, on our breasts." Despite such dehumanizing treatment, most internees worked hard to control their bitterness. They created workable communities inside the camps and demonstrated again and again their loyalty as Americans.

These are but two of the many stories from history that can be found in the pages of the Lucent Books World History series. All World History titles rely on sound research and verifiable evidence, and all give students a clear sense of time, place, and chronology through maps and timelines as well as text.

All titles include a wide range of authoritative perspectives that demonstrate the complexity of historical interpretation and sharpen the reader's critical thinking skills. Formally documented quotations and annotated bibliographies enable students to locate and evaluate sources, often instantaneously via the Internet, and serve as valuable tools for further research and debate.

Finally, Lucent's World History titles present rousing good stories, featuring vivid primary source quotations drawn from unique, sometimes obscure sources such as diaries, public records, and contemporary chronicles. In this way, the voices of participants and witnesses as well as important biographers and historians bring the study of history to life. As we are caught up in the lives of others, we are reminded that we too are characters in the ongoing human saga, and we are better prepared for our own roles.

Important Dates in

1948
The South African government begins to systematically implement an official policy of strict racial segregation and discrimination called apartheid.

1969
American astronauts Neil Armstrong and Edwin "Buzz" Aldrin become the first humans to walk on the moon.

1960
South African police fire into a crowd of blacks demonstrating against pass laws in the township of Sharpeville, killing sixty-nine and wounding 180.

1967
Six-Day War between Israel and the Arab nations of Egypt, Syria, and Jordan.

1950 1955 1960 1965 1970

1957
The space age begins as the Soviet Union launches the first artificial satellite, *Sputnik I,* into Earth's orbit.

1963
U.S. president John F. Kennedy is assassinated in Dallas, Texas.

1972
Palestinian terrorists attack the Winter Olympic Games in Munich, Germany, killing nine Israeli athletes.

1964
A South African court finds African National Congress (ANC) leader Nelson Mandela guilty of sabotage and sentences him to life in prison.

South African Apartheid

1976
Civil unrest spreads throughout South Africa after police fire on black schoolchildren in the Soweto township.

1977
Journalist and outspoken opponent of apartheid Stephen Biko dies after a series of brutal beatings administered while in police custody.

1984
World's worst industrial disaster occurs as an accidental release of chemicals from the Union Carbide plant in Bhopal, India, kills fifteen thousand and injures hundreds of thousands.

1986
Two major disasters shock the world as a nuclear reactor blows up at Chernobyl in the Soviet Union and the space shuttle *Challenger* explodes on takeoff in Florida.

1989
The Berlin Wall, symbol of Communist oppression, is torn down as communism collapses in Eastern Europe.

1989
F.W. de Klerk is named prime minister of South Africa and begins negotiations with antiapartheid leaders.

1990
The ban outlawing the ANC is lifted, Nelson Mandela is released from prison, and many apartheid laws are abolished or no longer enforced.

1994
Nelson Mandela is inaugurated as South Africa's first democratically elected president.

1975 1980 1985 1990 1995 2000

Introduction

A Triumph of the Human Spirit

In 1966 a five-year-old boy living near Johannesburg, South Africa, found a torn page of a magazine blown up against a fence. Mark Mathabane was then too young to understand the word *apartheid,* yet the grim reality of its meaning would soon be made clear to him. The pictures in the magazine showed beautiful homes belonging to white people—homes far nicer than anything he had ever seen in the ghetto where he lived. Mathabane took the pictures home. He showed them to his mother and told her that, when he grew up, he would build her a nice house like the ones in the magazine.

His mother asked him what made him think he could do that. "I'll have lots of money, so it will be easy," he confidently told her. "Even if you had all the money in the world, my child," she said gently, "you wouldn't build that house." When Mathabane asked why, her answer startled him. "Because," she said, "it's against the law for black people to own houses."[1]

For more than four decades the policy of strict racial separation and discrimination called apartheid—an Afrikaans word meaning "apartness"—crushed the dreams of nonwhite South Africans like Mark Mathabane. Racism has existed in all cultures in all times, but apartheid in South Africa was unique in the twentieth century because it was formal government policy, officially established and officially enforced. Beginning in 1948, every single person in the country was assigned a formal racial category—White, Asian (including Indians), Colored, or African. A person's civil rights and freedoms to work, reside, and travel depended on his or her racial category. Over time, as more and more laws were passed to ensure that the members of different races were separated from each other, the rights of all South Africans except Europeans were severely limited. In effect, the policy made inequality the law of the land. Those who questioned the law or worked against it risked imprisonment and even death.

Apartheid's intent was clear from the beginning. Hendrik Verwoerd, elected prime minister in 1958, stated what everyone knew to be the driving force behind the policy—restricting the rights of dark-skinned people, who formed the vast majority of South Africa's population, to ensure state control by the small white minority. "Our motto," he said, "is to maintain white supremacy for all time to come over our own people and our country, by force if necessary."[2] True to his word, Verwoerd approved the use of force during his administration—as did all other white South African administrations that followed. For more than forty years South Africa's police force and army crushed resistance to the harsh laws of apartheid. Thousands of people were killed and tens of thousands imprisoned or tortured.

But perhaps the worst effect of apartheid was the way it blunted the hopes of millions of nonwhite South Africans like Mark Mathabane, who grew up to write persuasively about the injustice of the policy. Although white South Africans of

As South Africa's prime minister in the 1960s, Hendrik Verwoerd vowed to maintain white supremacy, "by force, if necessary."

The "Chameleon Dance" of Apartheid

The absurdity of South Africa's racial classification laws and the immense amount of work that went into enforcing them can be inferred from a short news item in the Johannesburg Star *of March 21, 1986.*

More than 1,000 people officially changed color last year. They were reclassified from one race group to another by the stroke of a Government pen. Details of what is dubbed "the chameleon dance" were given in reply to Opposition question in Parliament. The minister of Home Affairs, Mr. Stoffel Botha, disclosed that:

- 702 colored people turned white
- 19 whites became colored
- One Indian became white
- Three Chinese became white
- 50 Indians became colored
- 43 coloreds became Indians
- 21 Indians became Malay
- 30 Malays went Indian
- 249 blacks became colored
- 20 coloreds became black
- Two blacks became "other Asians"
- One black was classified Griqua [tribe/ethnic group]
- 11 coloreds became Chinese
- Three coloreds went Malay
- One Chinese became colored
- Eight Malays became colored
- Three blacks were classified as Malay
- No blacks became white and no whites became black

Jonathan Paton, *The Land and People of South Africa.* New York: J.B. Lippincott, 1990, p. 29.

European descent made up only about 20 percent of the country's population, under apartheid the white minority controlled an estimated 87 percent of South Africa, including all major city governments, ports, industrial areas, mines, and prime farmland. Native Africans, on the other hand, could not own land or property outside impoverished, designated areas. They were poorly educated. They could not vote and were ineligible for well-paying jobs, and they were forbidden to marry outside their racial group.

The poverty and oppressive conditions that blacks endured bred resentment and anger that took many forms, including an antiapartheid movement that turned violent. The struggle to end apartheid was bitter and bloody. For decades supporters of apartheid resisted reform. But just when it appeared that South Africa would erupt into outright civil war, leading South Africans negotiated dramatic political change, and the apparatus of apartheid was dismantled with startling speed in 1994. Bishop Desmond Tutu, one of the architects of that seemingly miraculous turn of events, explained why he believed that the outcome represented one of the great triumphs of the human spirit: "I suppose that human beings looking at it would say that arms are the most dangerous things that a dictator, a tyrant needs to fear. But in fact, no—it is when people decide they want to be free. Once they have made up their minds to that, there is nothing that will stop them."[3]

An important combination of factors actually contributed to the end of apartheid. International human rights organizations sympathetic to South Africa's oppressed peoples mounted well-publicized campaigns to raise public awareness of apartheid's injustices. And economic boycotts and diplomatic pressure by governments around the world made it clear that the continuation of apartheid would entail crippling costs for South Africa's economy and leave South Africa an outcast state among world nations. Nevertheless, the story of apartheid is at its heart the story of a downtrodden people who, against high odds, won a great battle against oppression.

Chapter One

The Roots of Apartheid

Although apartheid was made official government policy in 1948, its roots go much deeper in South African history. For more than three hundred years, in fact, the relationship between whites and native South Africans was one of conquest, plunder, and oppression.

The pattern was established as early as 1652, when European traders of the Dutch East India Company built a small fort at the Cape of Good Hope, the point of land at the southern tip of the African continent. The fort was to serve as a kind of rest stop for ships traveling between European ports and the Far East. In this age of exploration, seafaring nations had discovered that a diet of fresh fruits and vegetables kept sailors from dying of scurvy on voyages that could take years. White settlers at the Cape supplied such fresh stores to the crews of ships who used the harbor. But the land around the Cape had been settled hundreds of years earlier by two native African peoples, the San and the Khoikhoi. As time went on, the white settlers began taking up more and more grazing land to grow their crops. Eventually war broke out, but because the Europeans had superior weapons the Khoikhoi were defeated and the San were virtually wiped out.

These victories provided the Dutch with abundant land—one of two main prerequisites for white prosperity in South Africa. The other was cheap labor. The need for these two resources—land and labor—arises again and again in South African history. It has motivated many of the racial laws passed by whites over the centuries. As the Dutch colony at the Cape grew in size during the 1600s, slaves were imported from Asia and other parts of Africa to work the land. The mingling of the slaves with the Dutch and the Khoikhoi produced a racially mixed people that white South Africans called "the Coloreds."

The Afrikaners

Meanwhile, white settlers were developing a unique culture of their own. Most settlers were Dutch, but some had come from Germany. A few had fled religious persecution in France. By 1775 there were fifteen thousand whites living in or near Cape Town. They called themselves Afrikaners because they spoke a Dutch-based language called Afrikaans. Almost all of them belonged to the Dutch Reformed Church, a Protestant sect whose members believed they were strictly following God's ways as set down in the Bible. One of the Afrikaners' most firmly held beliefs was that the races were meant to be kept separate and that the white race should rule over all others.

As time went on, rural Afrikaners called Boers (the Dutch word for "farmer")

pushed farther and farther inland from the Cape. As they did so, they clashed with other native African groups who spoke a language called Bantu. These Bantu-speaking tribes were moving into the country's interior from the north and east. For most of the nineteenth century the Boers and the Bantus warred against each other. Although the Boers suffered many defeats, in the end Bantu spears were no match for Boer guns.

But while the Boers were fighting the Bantus in the interior, unsettling developments were taking place at the coast—political upheaval that would fill Afrikaners with resentment for the better part of two centuries. In 1814, after a series of European wars, Britain took control of the Cape Town colony. Most Afrikaners did not welcome the prospect of becoming part of the British empire. Afraid they would be forced to give up their language, their slaves, and maybe even their religion, some of them organized a violent uprising against the British. The rebellion was crushed and five Boer rebels were hanged by the British in 1815, but the rebellion remained a potent symbol of the white South African independence movement.

In this nineteenth-century illustration, a family of Boer pioneers, or trekkers, rests during their Great Trek journey to prepare a meal.

A group of Boer trekkers journeys into a rugged valley as they make their way into the interior of South Africa.

The Great Trek

Unrest among Afrikaner residents of the Cape Colony reached new levels in 1833 when slavery was abolished in British colonies all over the world. The law angered Afrikaners, who had no intention of freeing their slaves. Their religion taught them that they were a chosen people who were meant to rule over races that they considered inferior. Convinced that their culture was under attack, many Boers decided it was time to leave the colony. In his book *A Traveller's History of South Africa*, David Mason described what happened next:

> Simmering resentment against British modes of rule boiled over in 1836 with the beginning of a mass migration of Boers away from the Cape and into the interior. Over the next six years, some 15,000 Afrikaners would join this exodus which differed in intention from any of the previous migrations of whites across southern Africa. It was a confusing occurrence, for the most part arduous, as families and communities packed up their belongings onto roughly constructed ox-wagons and headed in a north-easterly direction. Everything went with them including livestock and servants and chests crammed full of belongings . . . .
>
> Those who went had certain traits in common. There were few professional men on the trek for professional

A Titanic Resentment

Historian Brian Lapping claims that the impulse toward apartheid had its roots in the deep humiliation felt by Afrikaners over their relationship with Great Britain. Apartheid was a way for Afrikaners to show the world that no one would tell them how to run their own country:

The South African whites did not go wrong suddenly in 1948—or any other year. They did not go wrong because they are a uniquely evil or racist or authoritarian people. They went wrong because the experience of the previous three hundred years had brought them to a state of frustrated and enraged nationalist fervor that desperately needed a target. . . .

A person who has been humiliated at work and comes home to thrash the children is acting as Afrikaners did when they invented apartheid. The majority of Afrikaners—white South Africans who speak Afrikaans—developed a gnawing resentment against the British Empire, which had arrived uninvited at the start of the nineteenth century to rule what they considered their country. . . .

The British dominated the vast gold- and diamond-mining companies, the civil service, the professions, the army; they were the superior class. The Afrikaners were mostly farmers and, increasingly . . . they formed an underclass. The Afrikaners claimed with some cause that they had been dispossessed, deceived and brutally defeated by the British. (The fact that blacks could make a similar complaint with even more justification did nothing to alleviate the morose feelings of the Afrikaners.) They worked up a national resentment titanic in its bitterness.

Brian Lapping, *Apartheid: A History*. New York: George Braziller, 1987, p. xvi.

> men were able to make a good living under the British. Rather, those who went were mostly tradesmen, herders or agriculturists, self-reliant and steady folk used to looking out only for themselves and their families.[4]

This mass exodus of wagon trains pulled by oxen would forever after be known as the Great Trek, and the Afrikaners who took part in the migration would be called Voortrekkers ("pioneers") or "trekkers."

The trekkers' leader, Piet Retief, stated that one of the reasons they sought to escape British rule was their duty to "preserve the proper relations between master and servant."[5] As noted by Brian Lapping in his book *Apartheid: A History*, such relations were considered nonnegotiable: "The Afrikaners remained unwilling to have the British telling them what to do. Their republican ideals, derived from the Netherlands in the seventeenth century, were complemented by one overriding principle: the right of their white citizens to treat blacks as servants or slaves."[6] Accordingly, the trekkers took slaves and servants along with them on their journey into the interior of South Africa.

Just as westward-moving pioneers in nineteenth-century America encountered hostile native peoples already living on the land that the pioneers were intent on settling, the Afrikaners came into conflict with native Africans. The most formidable foes they faced were the fierce warriors of the Zulu tribe. Retief was killed in 1838 while trying to negotiate with the Zulu chief Dingaan. About five hundred of Retief's followers were wiped out soon afterward. The Afrikaners had their successes, too. At the Battle of Blood River—so named because the Ncome River was said to run red with blood—they killed three thousand Zulus without a single Afrikaner death.

Growing British Influence

By 1850 what would one day become South Africa was a patchwork of native kingdoms and more or less independent European colonies with little if any ability to defend themselves. Afrikaners who survived the Great Trek had set up two independent colonies, or Boer republics—the Orange Free State and the Transvaal. The Boers had good reason to feel embattled because both republics were surrounded by generally hostile African tribes. Meanwhile, the British retained control of two colonies: Cape Town and its surrounding lands and a coastal area to the northeast that was known as Natal. By the end of the nineteenth century, the British Empire had acquired control of all the native tribal kingdoms, either by treaty or conquest, which increased Boer fears that their republics too would be gobbled up by their British enemy.

Two unexpected developments in the second half of the century guaranteed that the Boers would not be left alone to create the kind of society they wanted. First, diamonds were discovered in the Orange Free State in 1867. Then, nineteen years later, gold was discovered in the Transvaal. As the news spread, miners and fortune hunters flocked to the region from all over the world. Most of them, however, were British, and soon the number of British inhabitants of the Boer republics actually outnumbered the Boers. Yet the Boers, whose dislike of the British had only intensified, refused to allow anyone other than Boers citizenship or voting rights.

Eventually Britain moved to take control of the vast wealth in Boer hands. In 1899, following a failed British attempt to create a civil uprising in the Transvaal, the Boer War broke out. Within a year close to a half-million British troops were battling only ninety thousand Boers. The badly outnumbered Boers resorted to guerrilla warfare—sabotage, ambush, and terror tactics—but lost their bloody struggle in 1902. Surviving Boers were greatly embittered by the British war strategy, devised by Lord Kitchener, of systematically destroying farms and farmland and of confining civilians (both blacks and whites) in specially built concentration camps under brutal conditions of deprivation and disease. In *South Africa: A Narrative History,* historian Frank Welsh sums up the grim legacy of Kitchener's policy:

> All country dwellers who might, willingly or not, support the commandos [Boer guerrilla fighters] were rounded up and housed in refugee or "concentration" camps. . . . More than twenty thousand Boer women and children died in the concentration camps. From a population of perhaps half a million, this was a terrifying proportion. Fighters do not find it too difficult to forgive those they have met in battle, but the deaths of so many innocents left a bitterness that has not yet disappeared a century later.[7]

Shrinking Rights

While the British and the Boers were fighting for control of the country's mineral riches, nonwhite South Africans were struggling for basic human rights. South Africa's population included substantial numbers of Indians and other Asian immigrants who, like native blacks, were harshly discriminated against by the white majority. Beginning in 1894, a young Indian lawyer named Mohandas Gandhi (destined to lead India's independence movement decades later, but unknown at the time) led a series of nonviolent protests against white rule in Africa. Gandhi, who had studied law in London, had experienced discrimination firsthand a week after his arrival in South Africa. He had purchased a first-class train ticket from Durban to Pretoria but, despite his well-dressed appearance and educated manners, a white passenger objected to sharing a compartment with him. A policeman then threw Gandhi off the train. At the time, Asians, like black Africans, were not allowed out of doors after nine o'clock at night and were not allowed to use the same footpaths that whites used. Although Gandhi lived in South Africa until 1914, his continuing objection to the discriminatory practices of white South Africans had little official effect.

In 1910, South Africa's four European colonies—the Cape Colony, Transvaal, Orange Free State, and Natal—became provinces in the newly created Union of South Africa, a federal state now officially a member of the British Commonwealth. Almost immediately, there were calls from nonwhites for greater representation in government and other democratic reforms. South African whites, both Afrikaners and former British colonial administrators, moved to protect their privileged status by passing laws restricting the rights of nonwhites.

First, virtually all nonwhites were prohibited from voting. Then, in 1911, the government banned strikes by black workers while restricting access to the best jobs to white workers only. In 1913 the Natives' Land Act was passed, officially setting aside 92.7 percent of the new country—including the best land and all the major towns—for whites only

The Natives' Land Act of 1913

Not long after South Africa became an independent nation in 1910, the white minority government began passing laws to segregate the races. The most important of these, according to David Mason, author of A Traveller's History of South Africa, *was the 1913 law ensuring that the country's best farmland could never be owned by blacks:*

Simply put, the Act outlawed the renting or purchase of land by Africans anywhere outside areas designated as reserved. The reserves covered a mere 7 percent of the land total of South Africa, this is 22 million acres, and were both removed from areas of white land ownership and deliberately placed away from the most desirable areas of agricultural commerce. Land was demarcated either as "white" or "native" and there could be no change between the two categories. So, in effect, African cultivators [farmers] were banned from some 93 percent of the land of the Union (or viewed another way, 67 percent of the population were restricted to 7 percent of the country's land mass).

David Mason, *A Traveller's History of South Africa.* New York: Interlink, 2004, p. 165.

In this 1928 photo, a black South African man stands outside his mud hut on a stretch of desolate, nonarable land.

and designating the remaining 7.3 percent as reserves to which the black population would be relocated. In addition to giving whites control of the most desirable land, the new laws guaranteed a source of cheap labor since the areas that nonwhites were restricted to could never support the people sent there. Few South African black miners would have chosen to work in the hot, dirty, dangerous, and disease-ridden environment of white-owned gold and diamond mines. The new laws, however, severely limited their opportunities to make a living any other way.

Birth of the African National Congress

In response to this repression, a small group of educated black Africans gathered in Bloemfontein, the capital of the Orange Free State, in January 1912. They were determined to organize formal opposition. The gathering was led by Pixley Seme, the most influential black man of his time. A member of the Zulu royal family, he was a lawyer who held degrees from both Columbia University in New York and Oxford University in England. Seme was also exceptionally self-assured and unafraid of confrontation (he once pulled a gun on whites who had threatened to have him thrown out of a railway car, forcing them to back down). Seme and his colleagues were outraged that, while their nation was now called the Union of South Africa, black people had no voice in that union and no say in how its laws were made. Seme argued that the time had come to create an organization dedicated to national unity and to defending the rights of all Africans.

The meeting marked the creation of the African National Congress (ANC). The first part of its mission, uniting all the different African peoples, was a huge undertaking that was likely to take decades. But members of the ANC believed that, if black Africans were ever to stand up to the white power structure, they would have to do so together. Sol Plaatje was chosen as the first leader of the ANC.

Among Plaatje's first priorities was protesting the Natives' Land Act. As Lapping notes, Plaatje had firsthand knowledge of the misery caused by forcing blacks to live in reserves and supply cheap labor for the mines:

> Plaatje, travelling on his bicycle in the Orange Free State, saw families whom farmers had evicted [as Plaatje writes] "living on the roads, their . . . flocks emaciated by lack of fodder, many of them dying while the wandering owners ran the risk of prosecution for travelling with unhealthy stock." These families did not know where they were going. They had no idea that once they reached the reserves the overcrowding there would drive thousands of their men to queue [line up] at the native labor office and, if lucky enough to be recruited, to walk to the Rand [the area of the Transvaal where gold was discovered, far from the reserves], there to live in barracks compounds and go down the mines.[8]

The gold miners had to live in communal barracks because black workers were not allowed to bring their families with them. In practice, being a gold or diamond miner was much like being in prison—although few prisoners worked as hard as miners. To prevent miners from smuggling gold or diamonds out of the mines, the mining companies built fenced-in compounds where black workers were required to eat and sleep during the hours they were not underground. It was an oppressive daily routine that, in the diamond mines, ended with one last indignity. When miners' work contracts ended and they were released to go home, they were kept naked in a separate compound for several days and their excrement thoroughly searched to make sure they did not attempt to smuggle raw diamonds by swallowing them.

In 1914 General J. B. M. Hertzog founded South Africa's National Party, whose aim was to maintain white supremacy.

Two Parties on a Collision Course

The ANC rallied grass-roots activism to battle against this oppression in the courts and legislatures. But in 1914 another political organization was born that, while also claiming to be battling injustice, had entirely different goals. Still bitter over continuing British influence in South Africa, Afrikaners (the descendants of the original Dutch settlers) formed the National Party (NP). J.B.M. Hertzog, a Boer War general and founder of the NP, believed that Afrikaners must govern the country and that people who did not speak Afrikaans or who had come from elsewhere would always be outsiders "who did not have the right love for South Africa."[9]

The NP was firmly based on the concept of white supremacy, so although its immediate quarrel was with the British, it had little sympathy for the goals of the ANC. Over the next three decades each group worked to unite its followers against perceived injustices. Two world wars, however, distracted South Africa from its internal problems. Not until World War II ended in 1945 was the stage set for a confrontation between the NP and the ANC—two organizations with sharply contrasting visions of what kind of country South Africa ought to be.

Chapter Two

A "Diabolical" Plan

The National Party (NP), rose to power in the mid-1920s and gained control of the South African government in 1948 after a lengthy power struggle with rival hard-line Afrikaner groups. The NP government, known as Nationalists, under Prime Minister D.F. Malan, quickly set about constructing a political and social system to ensure white supremacy for all time. Discrimination had always been part of South African society, but the new system, called apartheid, took discrimination to an unprecedented level. Apartheid law was specifically designed to determine and control South Africans' lives from cradle to grave. African National Congress (ANC) leader Nelson Mandela, who was imprisoned for twenty-seven years for his antiapartheid activities, wrote that apartheid

> represented the codification in one oppressive system of all the laws and regulations that kept Africans in an inferior position to whites for centuries. . . . The often haphazard segregation of the past three hundred years was to be consolidated into a monolithic system that was diabolical in its detail, inescapable in its reach and overwhelming in its power.[10]

In 1943, during World War II, Mandela, along with Oliver Tambo and Walter Sisulu, had formed the Youth League of the ANC. These three young leaders wholeheartedly agreed with the ANC's goals of a democratic, nonracial society. But they also favored confrontational means to reach that goal—demonstrations such as mass marches, boycotts, and strikes. Immediately after the war they were buoyed by knowledge of the defeat of Nazi Germany—the most brutal racist regime in history—and the birth of the United Nations, which raised their hopes that the world at large would no longer tolerate racial discrimination as official policy.

A Pivotal Election

But the NP victory in the general election of 1948 proved a nasty surprise for anyone who hoped that the nation's discriminatory practices might ease. The NP's campaign had concentrated on a single theme: "racial purity"[11] through continued white dominance. According to the NP platform, Indians and other Asians who lived in the country would be declared permanent aliens and encouraged to return to their countries of origin whenever possible. Blacks were to be considered temporary visitors to white areas and would otherwise be restricted

Oliver Tambo (left), Nelson Mandela (below), and Walter Sisulu (below left) challenged the apartheid system by organizing a series of boycotts, marches, and strikes.

to reserves. No nonwhite Africans would ever have the chance to gain political or social rights equal to those of whites.

That message resonated strongly with white voters alarmed by an influx of blacks moving into the cities because making a decent living in the reserves was so hard. The black migration to the cities raised fears among whites that they would lose their jobs to black workers. Meanwhile, mine owners, factory owners, and farmers, concerned about black workers' demands for better wages, feared that their source of cheap labor was about to dry up. The NP promised a solution to the problem: Nonwhites would be put in their place and a system devised to ensure they stayed there. That simple promise swayed enough anxious white voters to the NP's side for the party to win power (blacks, of course, could not take part in the election).

Afrikaners, while only 12 percent of the population, dominated Malan's new government, in part because soon after the election the NP passed a law that required all civil servants to speak both English and Afrikaans. Since few non-Afrikaner English-speakers bothered to learn Afrikaans, the law effectively ensured that the vast majority of government workers would always be Afrikan-

A Universally Offensive System

In his study of postapartheid South Africa, Sebastian Mallaby describes how South Africa's obsession with apartheid exceeded the kind of racism historically practiced in most countries:

Racism exists everywhere, but no regime since Hitler's has espoused it quite so blatantly. . . . No other society has erected so complicated a legal scaffolding to support discrimination, and thereby appeared so universally offensive. South Africa's Population Registration Act, the keystone of apartheid, required that the race of each South African be registered at birth. . . . To determine borderline cases, bureaucrats scrutinized fingernails, peered at nostrils, and tested the curliness of people's hair by running pencils through it.

White South Africans built a vast edifice of privilege on these spurious distinctions. They reserved for themselves the best jobs, the best schools, nearly all the land and all political power. They bulldozed entire black suburbs, because they disliked having black communities living too near white ones. Those who resisted were treated viciously. Policemen gassed and whipped children at rally after rally in the black townships.

Sebastian Mallaby, *After Apartheid: The Future of South Africa.* New York: Times Books, 1992, p. 5.

ers. Afrikaners also began moving into the police force and the military in great numbers; officers who opposed Afrikaner policies were replaced whenever possible. With the government and security forces firmly in their control, hard-line Afrikaner segregationists were free to implement their vision of a society divided rigidly along racial lines.

Afrikaners also felt that, by building a society to their own specifications, they were affirming their culture and at least symbolically throwing off the hated British rule. There was a strong sense that they had finally won what was rightfully theirs. As Malan announced after the election, "For the first time since Union, South Africa is our own."[12]

The Pillars of Apartheid

The system of apartheid that the NP began constructing in 1948 rested on four basic principles. The first was the categorization of the nation's people into one of four official "racial groups"[13]—White, Asian, Colored, or African. At this time, the population was approximately 12 percent White, 3 percent Asian, 8 percent Colored (or mixed race), and 77 percent African (or black). Second, as the only "civilized" race, whites were to exercise complete political power over all other races. The third principle was that white interests always outweighed nonwhite interests—the state did not have to provide equal, separate facilities for other races.

Finally, all whites, no matter where they came from, were classified as White. Black Africans, however, were further divided (and therefore rendered less powerful) into nine tribal subgroups, each linked to a supposed "homeland." South Africans of Indian and Asian descent, even if their families had lived in South Africa for hundreds of years, were considered aliens and were encouraged to return to their land of origin.

The period from 1948 to 1959—when long-held Afrikaner notions about the need for segregation of the races became law—are sometimes called the years of *baaskaap* apartheid. *Baaskaap* means "boss-ship" in Afrikaans. It refers to the core belief underlying all apartheid laws: that whites had a God-given right, in fact a duty, to rule over all other South Africans. Hendrik Verwoerd, the supremely confident Afrikaner politician widely credited as the main architect of apartheid, once wrote that perhaps Afrikaners had been divinely sent to South Africa so that "all that has been built up since the days of Christ may be maintained for the good of all mankind."[14]

Segregation Legislation

During its first two years in power, the NP government passed a flurry of restrictive laws that few if any non-Afrikaners could view as being "for the good of all mankind." The racist basis of those laws is clear in a letter Malan wrote to a Christian minister in the United States who had asked him to justify apartheid. Malan's response revealed the deep-seated fears and paranoia fundamental to racism:

> The difference in color is merely the physical manifestation of the contrast

> between two irreconcilable ways of life, between barbarism and civilization, between heathendom and Christianity, and finally between overwhelming numerical odds on the one hand and insignificant numbers on the other. . . .
>
> From the outset the European colonists were far out-numbered; there is no doubt that if they had succumbed to the temptation of assimilation, they would have been submerged in the Black heathendom of Africa as effectively as if they had been completely annihilated. Of necessity they had to arm and protect themselves against this ever-growing menace, and how could it better be done than by throwing an impenetrable armor around themselves—the armor of racial purity and self-preservation.[15]

The high priority most Afrikaners gave "racial purity" explains the speed with which several cruel pieces of legislation were passed. The Prohibition of Mixed Marriages Act and the Immorality Act, both enacted in 1949, prohibited whites from marrying or having sexual relations with people of other racial groups. At a pen stroke, marriages between people in different groups were declared illegal. Thousands of married couples were forced to petition the courts to get one spouse or the other reclassified. If unsuccessful, they could not live together without risking imprisonment.

Another law that caused great hardship was the Population Registration Act of 1950. According to Welsh the "basic weapon"[16] of apartheid, this law not only classified every individual by racial group but required each person to carry an identity card stating that classification. This requirement had serious implications. Despite its history of white separatism, South Africa had long been a mixed-race society, and determining a person's race was not simple, certainly not a matter of appearance alone. For example, was the daughter of a Colored man and an Indian woman to be considered Indian or Colored? Apartheid law dictated that a Racial Classification Board be created to resolve thousands of such complexities. The process was inherently unfair and caused much misery: In one instance, Beck explains, students at a school in the Transvaal complained that a girl "looked colored."[17] Although her parents were classified as white Afrikaners, she was reclassified as Colored and forced out of school. Records show that the board arbitrarily shifted people from one racial class to another, in effect deciding their future.

The Group Areas Act of 1950 physically separated the races defined by the Population Registration Act. It created residential districts in cities where the races were segregated and provided for the forced removal of people found to be living in the "wrong" district.

Resettlement at Gunpoint

The future was particularly bleak for Africans affected by the Native Resettlement Act. This 1956 law nullified exist-

Under apartheid, all South Africans were required to carry a pass book like this one, which clearly indicated to which racial group a person belonged.

ing property rights for nonwhites. Blacks who had owned land in urban areas for decades or longer were ordered to move because their land had been zoned for whites only. Indians too were forced to sell their homes and shops in desirable neighborhoods of urban centers like Johannesburg and move to designated areas on the outskirts of town. Under this act millions of blacks were relocated far away from their former homes. Those who still had jobs in the city then had to make long, expensive commutes to work. It was not unusual for black workers to get up at two or three in the morning to catch a bus for an hours-long trip into a city that was once their home, only to make the same exhausting trip at the end of every workday.

One of the most notorious mass removals occurred in the township of Sophiatown, near Johannesburg. Blacks there were removed to a bleak place outside Johannesburg known as Soweto (South Western Townships). As Leonard Thompson notes in his history of South

The residents of this section of Sophiatown were allowed to stay put under the terms of the Native Resettlement Act because their homes were far from white homes.

Africa, such moves to the euphemistically called homelands were conducted with great brutality:

> The government claimed that these removals were voluntary. In fact, it intimidated the victims and when they resisted used force. An African woman who had been moved to a Homeland told an interviewer: "When they came to us, they came with guns and police. . . . They did not say anything, they just threw our belongings in [the government trucks]. . . . We did not know, we still do not know this place. . . ." And when we came here, they dumped our things, just dumped our things so that we are still here. What can we do now, we can do nothing.[18]

The disruption and destruction of once-thriving black communities like Sophiatown led to increased poverty, crime, and hopelessness, particularly among young black men who could see that they would have little chance to earn a decent living under apartheid. In addition to forcibly removing blacks from their homes in cities, the government instituted measures to make sure that whites would have as little contact with nonwhites as humanly possible. Segregation was the rule in all public places. "Whites Only" and "Nonwhites Only" signs appeared in shops, restaurants, and on buses and trains—even park benches were segregated.

Fighting "Communists"

The imposition of such harsh laws inevitably led to protests by Africans, Asians, Coloreds, and some whites. In typical heavy-handed fashion, the government responded by making virtually any public opposition a crime. It did so largely through the Suppression of Communism Act of 1950. Fiercely anti-Communist, Malan's administration not only outlawed the Communist Party of South Africa with this law, but by defining opposition of nearly any kind as "communism," criminalized legitimate dissent. Like Martin Luther King's followers in the American civil rights movement of the next decade, South Africans fighting for justice were called Communists and persecuted as national security threats. In this Cold War atmosphere,

Low Expectations

Speaking before Parliament in 1954, Minister of Native Affairs Hendrik Verwoerd outlined his plans for black education. His speech made it abundantly clear that, in his view, teachers of black students—or "Bantus" as he preferred to call all blacks—should hold the same low expectations of their pupils that he held:

The Bantu teacher must be integrated as an active agent in the process of the development of the Bantu community. He must learn not to feel above his community, with a consequent desire to become integrated into the European community. He becomes frustrated and rebellious when this does not take place, and he tries to make his community dissatisfied because of such misdirected ambitions which are alien to his people. . . . The Bantu must be guided to serve his own community in all respects. There is no place for him in the European community above the level of certain forms of labor. Within his own community, however, all doors are open. For that reason it is of no avail for him to receive a training which has as its aim absorption in the European community, where he cannot be absorbed.

In Nancy L. Clark and William H. Worger, *South Africa: The Rise and Fall of Apartheid.* London: Pearson Longman, 2004, p. 51.

anti-Communist European and American leaders were not likely to object to South Africa's human rights abuses because the government claimed to be fighting communism.

Ironically, under apartheid the South African minister of justice had nearly as much power to curtail human freedoms as the Communist dictators he officially condemned. The government further silenced dissent by declaring acts of civil disobedience to be crimes and by censoring virtually any speech or writing critical of apartheid. To enforce these policies against what it anticipated would be strong internal opposition,

Under the Bantu Education Act of 1953, mission schools such as this one were shut down and inferior public schools opened in their place.

Malan's government also built the best equipped and best trained army and police force in Africa.

Education and Apartheid

Led by Minister of Native Affairs Verwoerd, a man Welsh describes as "terrifyingly sincere,"[19] the Afrikaner creators of apartheid developed an amazingly thorough vision of what a proper society should be. The education system they devised may have had the most devastating long-term consequences of any part of apartheid's elaborate apparatus. In their eyes, education should train children solely for their role in life. The government, therefore, saw no point in teaching black children skills that would never be used in white-ruled South Africa. "Education," declared Verwoerd, "must train and teach people in accordance with their opportunities in life."[20] Under apartheid, the only function foreseen for blacks who ventured into white society was to work as cheap laborers, so teaching them even basic literacy was viewed as a waste of resources.

Until the beginning of apartheid, the schooling of black South Africans had been left almost exclusively to church missions. That troubled National Party leaders, who worried that some religious messages about equality and freedom might inspire black children to become rebellious adults. A second drawback of mission schools, according to the NP, was that there were not enough of them: The South African economy was expanding and these schools were not training enough black Africans to supply farms, businesses, and industrial concerns with a ready workforce.

As always, the solution to the problem was sought in new legislation. Under the Bantu Education Act of 1953, the government established a state-run system of schools just for nonwhite pupils. The state selected and trained teachers and decided which courses should be taught.

On the surface, this new policy appeared to benefit blacks. More African children were enrolled in schools than ever before.

Local languages were acceptable in the lower grades, but, unlike in white schools, those few children who managed to stay in school until the higher grades were taught Afrikaans and English so they would be better able to understand the demands of white employers once they reached adulthood.

But the system was deeply flawed. The curriculum was designed along racist principles, to suit the "nature and requirements of the black people." That is, black children were to be taught only the skills they would need among people in their own homelands or as laborers under white bosses. The education that the black students received was inferior in every way to that offered to white children. Attendance was not mandatory. Buildings and classrooms were shoddily built, books were often nonexistent, and teachers were poorly trained and poorly paid. In fact, the government spent up to ten times as much on education for white children. The majority of Africans regarded so-called Bantu education as a cruel farce. One measure of how poor that education was can be found in the number of African children who went on to college after the imposition of apartheid. Of 200,000 African children who entered the apartheid-inspired school system in 1950, only 400 passed the university entrance exams in 1962.

Turning Point

For apartheid advocates like Verwoerd, of course, those numbers were neither a surprise nor a concern. At a time when many world governments were bowing to civil rights movements, abolishing segration and racial discrimination, South Africa chose a course that led in the opposite direction. Not long after coming to power, the National Party committed itself to extending segregation into every corner of South African society.

Paradoxically, in doing so the government disregarded its own policy studies. In 1946 Prime Minister Jan Smuts had appointed an independent commission to study race relations—which he considered the most divisive political issue facing the nation—in light of South Africa's shifting demographics. Smuts hoped to get support for his position that blacks and whites should be rigidly separated. But his Native Laws Commission concluded in 1948 that the racial segregation of the entire society was neither feasible nor wise. If the country were to prosper in the long term, whites and nonwhites would have to learn to live and work together. The commission also concluded that the massive costs of maintaining strict racial segregation were certain to be a huge drag on the economy. Refusing to heed such warnings, the government went ahead with its apartheid plans, and South Africa was plunged into a dark era.

Chapter Three

Resistance and Repression

While the National Party (NP) government forged ahead with its elaborate plan to embed racism into the fabric of South African life in the early 1950s, there was an upsurge in mass protests by blacks, Asians, and a few sympathetic whites. The opposition was led by the African National Congress (ANC).

During its first years in power, the National Party passed a number of segregation laws that were known in general, according to historian Dougie Oakes, as "petty apartheid."[21] Such laws were called petty because they were humiliating and unfair but in fact were little more than official codification of the many small ways discrimination had been practiced in South Africa for decades. Under petty apartheid laws, taxis, ambulances, parks, maternity wards, graveyards, sidewalks, and even parking spaces at drive-in movies were segregated according to race. Another example of petty apartheid was the law that reserved portions of all trains for white passengers. Blacks or Asians who did not remain in the sections assigned to them were subject to arrest and imprisonment.

As the largest and most visible organization opposing apartheid, the ANC attracted thousands of new members after the Population Registration Act and the Group Areas Act were passed, marking a new phase in the development of petty apartheid. These laws were more than humiliating—they provided the mechanisms for massive social dislocation and oppression. Their intent was to rigidly segregate South African society and forever deny nonwhites political and economic rights granted to whites.

Black and mixed-race South Africans made up the bulk of the ANC membership, but the organization was open to all races, and Indians, Asians, and whites who believed in racial equality were also members. Indeed, Indians were a strong

Mohandas Gandhi served as an inspiration to ANC leaders, who employed the Hindu independence leader's civil disobedience tactics to bring an end to apartheid.

presence within the ANC, whose early attempts to fight back against apartheid owed much to the spirit of Mohandas Gandhi, the champion of Indian independence whose activism had taken shape in South Africa. Gandhi's philosophy of nonviolent civil disobedience had proven successful in India and inspired millions around the world to protest human rights abuses by oppressive governments.

The Defiance Campaign

In the early 1950s the ANC planned boycotts of white businesses and what historians Nancy L. Clark and William H. Worger describe as "stay-at-home days"[22] on which students and workers refused to go to school or work. These protests were nonviolent, according to Gandhi's principles of civil disobedience.

The ANC's biggest early success was the Defiance Campaign of 1952, which originated with a letter from the ANC to Prime Minister Malan asking him to repeal several recently passed laws, including the so-called pass laws, perhaps the most universally hated of all the new apartheid measures.

At first only black men had been required to carry the official documents known as passes. But the 1952 laws replaced simple passbooks with ninety-six-page reference books that all black South African adults had to carry at all times or risk criminal charges and arrest. Passes included a photograph and records of the holder's employment history, tax payments, and any encounters with police.

In addition, pass laws forbade black people from leaving rural areas without an official permit from local authorities, and blacks were required to apply for another permit to seek work within 72 hours of entering a city. The pass laws were quite useful to the government in making sure that "unauthorized" people stayed out of white areas. Each year more than one hundred thousand Africans were imprisoned for pass law violations. Enforcing such laws took an enormous toll on the South African economy, since maintaining the necessary police force, courts, jails, and administrative system was extremely costly.

The Defiance Campaign began after the ANC's request to repeal apartheid laws was rejected. The campaign's goal was to embarrass the government by forcing it to arrest thousands of peaceful demonstrators. In preparation, volunteers attended meetings where they prayed and were trained not to retaliate with violence, no matter what the police did. Then the protesters purposely went to places where they were prohibited, refused to leave, and simply allowed themselves to be arrested. Nelson Mandela, then a thirty-four-year-old lawyer and the chief organizer of the Defiance Campaign, was arrested for violating curfew in Johannesburg (where blacks were not allowed outside after eleven at night). Other ANC volunteers were imprisoned after entering "Whites Only" areas of post offices, train stations, and restaurants.

At first, enthusiasm for the campaign swept the country. Many nonwhites saw it as a chance to finally strike a blow against oppression. As jails filled with thousands of volunteers, the South African government was exposed to unfavorable coverage in newspapers around the world. Meanwhile, membership in the ANC jumped from seven thousand to more than one hundred thousand. The police, however, became increasingly violent in their attempts to stop the demonstrations. Although the volunteers did not retaliate, enraged bystanders sometimes did. After a number of riots that caused the deaths of both police and bystanders, the ANC ended the campaign early in 1953.

The Defiance Campaign had two significant effects: The world recognized

In the early 1950s Nelson Mandela led the Defiance Campaign, in which protesters entered "Whites Only" areas and then refused to leave.

that the ANC had strong organizational and motivational ability, and the NP government realized that Nelson Mandela was a potential threat, capable perhaps of rallying international opposition to apartheid. The success of the campaign also boosted Mandela's self-confidence. As he wrote later, it freed him "from any lingering doubt or inferiority I might have still felt. . . . I could walk upright like a man, and look everyone in the eye with the dignity that comes from not having succumbed to oppression and fear."[23]

Making Dissent Illegal

As Mandela became more prominent politically, the government tried to clamp down on him and other ANC leaders, claiming authority under the Suppression of Communism Act. Ironically, Mandela and a number of other ANC leaders were themselves anti-Communist, but the law was written so broadly that any antigovernment sentiment was a prosecutable offense, and their actual political views were irrelevant.

The government soon hit on a better technique than imprisoning dissidents, which increased sympathy for their cause and damaged South Africa's international image. Instead, the government began to ban opposition leaders like Mandela from holding political offices, making political speeches, or even meeting with anyone other than their families. Hundreds of ANC, Indian, and trade union leaders were banned. It was an effective way to cripple organizations by preventing leaders from leading.

Although Mandela was subject to such bans for most of the 1950s, he still managed to continue the fight against apartheid. Since he suspected that the ANC itself, as well as other opposition groups, risked being banned, he set up a secret system by which leaders could communicate with each other through people unknown to the government. In 1953, during a brief period when Mandela was not banned, he spoke to a group of black workers who wanted to form a union as a way to insist on their rights:

> If you are not allowed to have your meetings publicly, then you must hold them over your machines in the factories, on the trams and buses as you travel home. You must have them in your villages and shanty towns. You must make every home, every shack and every mud structure where our people live, a branch of the trade union movement, and you must *never surrender*.[24]

The Freedom Charter

Mandela's secret networks and the ANC's organizational abilities led to a defining moment in the battle against apartheid on June 26, 1955. On that day three thousand delegates from all over South Africa met in Kliptown, a village near Johannesburg. Since top ANC leaders had already been banned, preparations for this Congress of the People were made by citizens as yet unknown to the authorities. Otherwise, the police would not have allowed the meeting to take place. The purpose of the meet-

A Freedom Fighter Convention

In his autobiography, Nelson Mandela writes that being arrested and imprisoned for treason had unexpected benefits for the antiapartheid movement:

We stayed in the Fort [the prison in Johannesburg] for two weeks, and despite the hardships, our spirits remained extremely high. We were permitted newspapers and read with gratification of the waves of indignation aroused by our arrests. Protest meetings and demonstrations were being held throughout South Africa; people carried signs declaring "We Stand by Our Leaders." We read of protest around the world over our incarceration.

Our communal cell became a kind of convention for far-flung freedom fighters. Many of us had been living under severe restrictions, making it illegal for us to meet and talk. Now, our enemy had gathered us all together under one roof for what had become the largest and longest unbanned meeting . . . in years. Younger leaders met older leaders they had only read about. Men from Natal mingled with leaders from the Transvaal. We reveled in the opportunity to exchange ideas and experiences for two weeks while we awaited trial.

. . . Every day, Vuyisile Mine, who years later was hanged by the government for political crimes, led the group in singing freedom songs. . . . We sang at the top of our lungs, and it kept our spirits high.

Nelson Mandela, *Long Walk to Freedom: The Autobiography of Nelson Mandela.* Boston: Little, Brown, 1994, p. 175.

ing was to draft a declaration in positive terms that spelled out the aims of the antiapartheid movement. Til now, the ANC's demands had been phrased in mostly negative terms, condemning apartheid and calling for its abolition. While the ANC naturally opposed the oppression inherent in enforcing apartheid, the rest of the world had little idea what the organization actually stood for.

The Freedom Charter drawn up by the Congress of the People was a remarkable document that remained a rallying point for antiapartheid forces for decades. In clear and unambiguous language it envisioned a free and fair society—a society radically different from the one envisioned by apartheid advocates. Among its provisions it stated:

> We, the people of South Africa, declare for all our country and the world to know:

A Five-Year Farce

According to historian Frank Welsh, the fair-mindedness of the judges at the Treason Trial produced the exact opposite of the result the government expected:

The Nationalist government hoped to seal its authority in a spectacular mass trial which began in December 1956 with the arrest of 150 prominent resisters of all races and communities. Originated by the former Nazi, now Minister of Justice, the usually competent Oswald Pirow, the hearing should have been an expertly arranged show trial, along the lines of those in Nazi Germany or communist Russia, demonstrating the abominable intentions of the vile accused. As it turned out, the five-year trial was indeed a long-running public show, but one in which the advantage was entirely with the accused. The prosecution degenerated into farce, as first one group and then others were discharged for want of evidence. The original high standards of the South African judicial system were again seen to have survived when in March 1962 the solemn Mr. Justice Rumpff, who had tried Sisulu and Mandela nine years before, gave a thoughtful summing-up which concluded with finding all the accused not guilty.

Frank Welsh, *South Africa: A Narrative History.* New York: Kodansha, 1999, p. 453.

In 1956 the South African government tried unsuccessfully to level charges of treason against Nelson Mandela and 155 other activists.

That South Africa belongs to all who live in it, black and white, and that no government can justly claim authority unless it is based on the will of all the people;

Every man and woman shall have the right to vote for and to stand as a candidate for all bodies which make laws;

There shall be equal status in the bodies of the state, in the courts and in the schools for all national groups and races;

The preaching and practice of national, race or color discrimination and contempt shall be a punishable crime.[25]

Although the government was apparently caught off guard by the Congress of the People, it reacted to the declaration immediately, launching an eighteen-month investigation of the meeting and its organizers. Then, in an early morning raid in December 1956, police arrested 156 people, including Mandela, and jailed them in a prison in Johannesburg. Most of the detainees were black, but there were twenty-three whites, twenty-one Indians, and seven people of mixed race in the group. After it announced that it had uncovered a vast conspiracy to commit violence against the state, the government charged the arrestees with treason and with being Communists.

The Treason Trial

The trial of the Congress of the People arrestees lasted for five years and became internationally famous as the Treason Trial. It was a fiasco for the government. The dignity and eloquence of the defendants—Mandela in particular—stood in sharp contrast to the hysterical charges made against them.

The low point, from a prosecution standpoint, may have come during the testimony of prosecution witness Professor Andrew Murray. A self-proclaimed expert on communism, Murray claimed that an analysis of the words used in ANC documents proved that its leaders were Communists. A defense lawyer asked Murray on the witness stand if he could definitely identify an author's politics just by the words used in a document. Murray said that he could, and the lawyer then read aloud a list of words from a book. When Murray said that he was sure the author was a Communist, the lawyer revealed that the book in question had been written by Murray himself. Embarrassing exchanges like this led the prosecutors to drop charges against most of the accused. By March 1961, only thirty of the defendants remained to face charges of treason.

Mandela was the primary spokesperson for those who remained, and he used the trial as a platform to educate the world about the ANC. When one of the judges asked him whether the freedom of blacks was a direct threat to Europeans, for example, he emphasized that, unlike the government, the ANC was not a racist organization:

No, it is not a direct threat to the Europeans, as Europeans. We are not anti-white; we are against white

> supremacy and in struggling against white supremacy we have the support of some sections of the European population. . . . As a matter of fact, My Lord, I think that we in the Congress must take credit for the fact that there is movement in this country for racial peace.[26]

Mandela's unshakable poise during the trial impressed even the prosecutors. When the three-judge panel announced their verdict, it was a blow to the state. They ruled that the government had failed to prove that the ANC was advocating a policy of violence. All defendants were found not guilty and allowed to go free. The trial, in effect, had greatly strengthened the ANC and the opponents of apartheid. In *Mandela: The Authorized Biography,* Anthony Sampson explains how its result was exactly the opposite of what the government intended:

> The long Treason Trial brought the various racial groups inside the courtroom much closer together. "I doubt whether we could have devised so effective a method of ensuring cohesion in resistance and of enlarging its embrace," said [Zulu chief Albert] Luthuli. "We didn't realize we had so much in common," said Paul Joseph, an Indian ex-factory worker from a humble background who became a friend of Mandela. "The trial created a cohesion that didn't exist before." The Africans found themselves pressed together with whites, Indians and Coloureds in roughly the same proportion as the population of the country. It was just the kind of multiracial partnership that many of them had been advocating. Whatever propaganda motives had led the government to bring the accused to trial, they could now spread their own counter-propaganda that this was a united, genuinely nonracial movement.[27]

Chapter Four

Grand Apartheid

In 1958 National Party (NP) prime minister J.G. Strijdom died in office and Hendrik Verwoerd, the minister of native affairs, became the new leader of South Africa. The determined and intolerant Verwoerd now had the power he needed to put his master plan of racial discrimination into practice—a plan that came to be called grand apartheid, in contrast to the specific small restrictions of petty apartheid laws. In its early stages, the harsh repression of grand apartheid seemed to have few harmful effects on the South African economy, but it did lead to violent civil unrest and even more violent reprisals that drove the anti-apartheid movement underground.

Verwoerd had an obsession with order. But the discrimination that had been practiced for so long in South Africa was part of a code of behavior that was largely unwritten. He set about making sure that, in the future, such discrimination would be given the force of law. The petty apartheid laws he had sponsored in his eight years as minister of native affairs were a start, but South African society was still far less segregated than he wished.

At this point blacks, whites, and Asians still sometimes worked together. Some blacks and Indians owned businesses in predominantly white areas and whites owned businesses in predominantly black and Indian areas. In some cities, nonwhites lived in close proximity to whites. In some social situations the races came into contact with each other. This was unacceptable to Verwoerd, who as minister of native affairs had done his best to eradicate what he called "Black spots"[28] like Johannesburg's Sophiatown.

Legalizing Racism

Now Verwoerd worked even harder to separate the races. The first law he signed as prime minister, and perhaps the most far-reaching, was the 1959 Promotion of Bantu Self Government Bill. Verwoerd called all blacks "Bantus" because it was the name of the group of languages that the original black South Africans spoke. He refused to call black people "Africans" or "natives" because he believed that Afrikaners were also native Africans. Regardless of which names were used, the bill was designed to splinter opposition to apartheid. It revised the classification of black Africans into eight ethnic groups, each assigned a self-governed homeland. (Eventually, the number of homelands would be increased to ten.) After the bill's passage, the government began forcibly removing millions of people from cities and towns—in many cases the only places they had ever lived—and virtually dumping them into homeland territory.

Sebastian Mallaby, author of *After Apartheid: The Future of South Africa*, asserts that another motivation for the homeland policy was simply to save money:

> [Blacks] without jobs in the rest of South Africa were legally confined to these poor patches of countryside and left to scratch a living from the land. For a time, the homelands and pass laws succeeded in their narrow aims. They saved the state the cost of paying out welfare benefits: the jobless and homeless could be dispatched to their huts. They saved industry the cost of decent wages: workers left their wives and children in the homeland, so employers paid only enough to support a single man.[29]

The establishment of self-governing tribal homelands—or Bantustans, as Verwoerd insisted they be called—was coupled with strict enforcement of the pass laws. This severely restricted the freedoms of South Africa's black citizens. It was easier than ever for police or security forces to arrest black people who were not where the government wanted them to be.

The Wind of Change

During the first half of 1960, two events drew worldwide attention to the degree of oppression imposed under apartheid. That February British prime minister Harold Macmillan paid an official visit to South Africa. Verwoerd entertained hopes that Macmillan would approve of apartheid—or at least not object publicly. He was severely disappointed. Appearing before the South African parliament in Cape Town, Macmillan made one of the most influential speeches ever delivered on the continent. He spoke approvingly of a "wind of change"[30] blowing through Africa:

> It has been our aim in the countries for which we have borne responsibility to create a society . . . in which men are given the opportunity to grow to their full stature—and that must in our view include the opportunity to have an increasing share in political power and responsibility [with] individual merit alone. . . . Our policy therefore is non-racial. It offers a future in which Africans, Europeans, Asians . . . will

Foreigners in Their Own Country

The establishment of "homelands," or Bantustans, was one of the most insidious aspects of apartheid. Historian Roger Beck describes how the National Party manipulated language to deny the majority of South Africans the freedom to move about their own country:

According to Verwoerd, there could be no racial discrimination against Africans in South Africa because there were no African citizens; African rights in White South Africa were not restricted because of race but because they were foreigners.

Of course, Africans had no say in the creation of the ethnicity-based *bantustans.* An African's ethnicity was anyway often difficult to determine because the various African ethnic groups had been intermarrying for centuries. And many Africans had never been near their assigned *bantustan,* having lived for generations on distant farms or in urban areas. All this mattered little to Verwoerd, however. To present an acceptable face to the world, he increasingly referred to "separate development" rather than apartheid; "Natives" became Bantu; *bantustans* became "homelands." Verwoerd envisioned a commonwealth of southern Africa to include the *bantustans* . . . and a [white] South African republic completely free of political ties to Great Britain.

Roger B. Beck, *The History of South Africa.* Westport, CT: Greenwood, 2000, p. 136.

Hendrik Verwoerd engineered a plan under which blacks were forced to live in tribal homelands, reducing black South Africans to the status of foreigners in their own country.

> all play their full part as citizens and in which feelings of race will be submerged in loyalty to new nations.[31]

Macmillan added that, since South Africa was a member of the British Commonwealth—sovereign states including the United Kingdom and several former British colonies—he would have liked to give it his full support and encouragement. However, the nation's apartheid policy made that impossible. Macmillan's speech was a huge incentive to South Africans of all races who opposed apartheid. For Verwoerd, however, it was an unpleasant surprise—particularly since the speech was broadcast live throughout the country. Verwoerd responded with defiance, declaring that white South Africans had the absolute right do whatever they felt necessary to ensure their survival.

Macmillan's rebuke was a blow to South Africa's international image, and an even worse blow was struck less than two months later. Impatient with the progress being made against apartheid, a group of young activists had broken away from the African National Con-

South Africa's leaders hoped that British prime minister Harold Macmillan would support South Africa's white supremacist policies, but he refused to do so.

When protesters converged on the police station in Sharpeville in 1960, officers opened fire, killing 69 and wounding another 180.

gress (ANC) in 1959 to form the Pan-Africanist Congress (PAC). On March 21, 1960, the PAC called for an Anti-Pass Day in some parts of the country. Demonstrators were asked to leave their passes at home and surrender themselves to the police. Like the ANC's Defiance Campaign of 1953, the demonstrations were intended to be nonviolent.

Massacre at Sharpeville

More than five thousand demonstrators converged on the police station in a township called Sharpeville, south of Johannesburg. Suddenly, and without warning, the police opened fire. Sixty-nine people were killed and 180 wounded—all but a few shot in the back. News of the Sharpeville massacre traveled swiftly around the world. It was condemned by the United States and at the United Nations. Huge crowds attended the victims' funerals, and the ANC organized a stay-at-home to mourn those killed. It was the first truly nationwide protest against the evils of apartheid.

Typically, Verwoerd responded to the outcry with increased repression. He insisted that the massacre was the fault of the protesters. The ANC and the PAC were declared illegal organizations, and the head of the ANC, along with eighteen thousand other people, was arrested under new emergency laws.

On April 8, in the midst of this turmoil, a deranged white farmer shot Verwoerd twice in the head. For a few days, it seemed possible that apartheid was going to lose its greatest champion. A new, potentially more moderate prime minister, some dared to hope, might take the country in a different direction.

Those hopes died a few months later when Verwoerd returned to office, seemingly as healthy as ever. His miraculous recovery—Verwoerd himself saw it as a sign from God—made him more popular than ever among Afrikaners. That popularity soared to new heights in 1961 when he withdrew South Africa from the British Commonwealth. Afrikaners had viewed Macmillan's "wind of change" speech of the year before as unwanted British meddling in South Africa's internal affairs. Withdrawal from the Commonwealth was welcomed as an appropriate response, as well as a proud declaration of the Afrikaners' determination to ignore the rest of the world while building their racist society.

Spear of the Nation: The ANC Takes Up Arms

With his authority now close to absolute, Verwoerd was more determined than ever to impose apartheid by force. His unswerving commitment to apartheid led leaders of the ANC and the PAC to a critical decision. The massacre of defenseless demonstrators at Sharpeville and the lack of government apology or accountability had convinced many of them that their policy of nonviolence was futile. At an ANC meeting in June 1961, Mandela reminded his followers of an old African proverb: "The attacks of the wild beast cannot be averted with only bare hands."[32]

Later that year both the ANC and the PAC formed militant wings to commit sabotage and other guerrilla attacks that would undermine the regime's operations. Their ultimate goal was to convince the white population of the need for change. Mandela was named commander in chief of the ANC militants, called Umkhonto we Sizwe (Spear of the Nation). The armed wing of the PAC was known as Poqo (which means "pure" or "alone"). Spear of the Nation launched its campaign of sabotage on December 16, 1961, with the detonation of about twenty bombs. That same day the group issued a leaflet, written by Mandela, that made clear the desperation that led to the decision to abandon nonviolence:

> The time comes in the life of any nation when there remain only two choices: submit or fight. That time has now come to South Africa. We shall not submit and we have no choice but to hit back by all means within our power in defense of our people, our future and our freedom. The government has interpreted the peacefulness of the movement as weakness; the people's non-violent policies have been taken as a green light for government violence. . . .
>
> We are striking out along a new road for the liberation of the people of this country. The government policy of

Mandela in Prison

Nelson Mandela's status as opposition leader was undiminished during his decades in prison. Biographer Anthony Sampson explains how prison life shaped Mandela's character and actually enhanced his powerful image:

Mandela's life sentence was a more serious test of his resilience than his two previous years in jail. He was now cut off from the world in his prime, at the age of forty-six, with no end in sight. . . . Now all the bright scenery and characters would contract into the single bare stage of his cell and the communal courtyard.

But there was a powerful consolation: he was not alone. With him were some of his closest friends, who could reinforce each other's morale and purpose, and develop a greater depth and self-awareness. At an age when most politicians tend to forget their earlier idealism in the pursuit of power, Mandela was compelled to think more deeply about his principles and ideas. In the microcosm of prison, stripped of all political trappings—platforms, megaphones, newspapers, crowds, well-tailored suits—and confined with his colleagues every day, he was able, as he put it, to stand back from himself, to see himself as others saw him. He learned to control his temper and strong will, to empathize and persuade, and to extend his influence and authority, not just over the other prisoners, but over the warders.

Anthony Sampson, *Mandela: The Authorized Biography*. New York: Knopf, 1999, p. 201.

Nelson Mandela sews prison clothing in the yard of Robben Island prison, where he was serving a life sentence on charges of sabotage.

> force, repression and violence will no longer be met with non-violent resistance only! The choice is not ours: it has been made by the Nationalist Government [the National Party] which has rejected every peaceable demand by the people for rights and freedom and answered every such demand with force and yet more force![33]

The ANC did not completely abandon its commitment to nonviolence, however. Spear of the Nation took great care at first to avoid the loss of human life. Bombs were placed to destroy buildings and electrical power stations, yet limit the damage to humans. Poqo was not as averse to killing—its leaders hoped to spark a mass uprising that would sweep the government from power. Members of Poqo led attacks on police stations and assassinated government officials.

A Losing Battle

Although both organizations successfully terrorized white Afrikaners, they proved little match for the state's heavily armed security forces. And they were unable to seriously disrupt the nation's economy. The bombings did not lead whites to call for the abandonment of the apartheid system—instead, they called for harsher treatment of any anti-apartheid activists who could be apprehended.

Under the ruthless direction of B.J. Vorster, Verwoerd's hard-line minister of justice, the government developed a huge network of paid informants, mostly blacks pressured to give information or desperate for cash. Vorster also oversaw the torture of hundreds of political prisoners. In a relatively short time, Vorster had the names of the leaders of Poqo and Spear of the Nation. By 1964 almost all militant leaders had been arrested and were awaiting trial.

Among them was Mandela. Following a raid on a farm near the Johannesburg suburb of Rivonia, he and eight other men were charged with sabotage, an offense that carried the death penalty. Mandela was chosen to give an opening speech to the court, explaining Spear of the Nation's aims and ideals. Although his lawyers strongly advised him to tone down the speech because it might cost him his life, Mandela refused. "I felt we were likely to hang no matter what we said, so we might as well say what we truly believed,"[34] he recalled later. Once again, his words transfixed a courtroom.

Defining the Struggle

Mandela's four-hour speech on April 24, 1964, was delivered with calmness and conviction before a profoundly quiet courtroom. At its conclusion, Mandela put down his notes, turned to face the judge, and spoke from memory:

> The ANC's struggle is a truly national one. It is a struggle of the African people, inspired by their own suffering and their own experience. It is a struggle for the right to live. During my lifetime I have fought against white domination, and I have fought against black domina-

Located just offshore near Cape Town, Robben Island Prison was where the South African government imprisoned those convicted of political crimes.

> tion. I have cherished the ideal of a democratic and free society in which all persons live together in harmony and with equal opportunities. It is an ideal which I hope to live for and to achieve. But if needs be, it is an ideal for which I am prepared to die.[35]

Mandela intended to back his words with action. He and fellow defendants Walter Sisulu and Govan Mbeki had agreed among themselves that they would not appeal the death sentence they expected. They feared that an appeal would be seen as an admission of weakness. "Our message," Mandela later recalled, "was that no sacrifice was too great in the struggle for freedom."[36] The defendants' humanitarian ideals and their courage resonated far beyond the borders of South Africa. Newspapers all over the world published sympathetic editorials.

A Police State

The international outcry might have had an effect on the judge. Instead of condemning Mandela and the principal defendants to death, as expected, he sentenced them to life imprisonment on

Robben Island, a penitentiary on an island off the shore of Cape Town. It was a victory of sorts, but with the ANC and the PAC effectively eliminated as political opposition groups, Verwoerd was free to proceed with his plans for grand apartheid. The pace of removal to the homelands was accelerated, pass laws were more strictly enforced, and the government increased its use of censorship. Virtually any speech or printed material that hinted at human equality was declared illegal.

South Africa was at this point a virtual police state—a nation ruled by brute force and an unjust legal system. New laws gave the government the power to arrest people secretly and then imprison them indefinitely without charges. The security forces were eventually expanded into the Bureau of State Security (BOSS). Its much-feared military-style units were composed of Afrikaners handpicked for their toughness. BOSS had an almost unlimited budget and, because it was allowed to operate in secret, very little accountability. Members of BOSS, notorious for their brutality and a legendary enjoyment of humiliating detainees, tortured and murdered unknown numbers of suspected antiapartheid activists.

Meanwhile, South Africa's economy was prospering during the 1960s—foreign investors, who recognized that the extremely low wages paid to nonwhite workers led to handsome profits, chose to overlook the injustices of apartheid. The core of Verwoerd's grand apartheid strategy was the belief that complete separation of the races would lead to stability, prosperity, and the ensured domination by the white race. With most antiapartheid leaders dead or in jail and the economy booming, it was easy for prospering whites to believe that he was right. Yet, despite the silencing of almost all internal opposition to apartheid, deep resentment was simmering beneath the surface—resentment that would make long-term stability under apartheid impossible.

Chapter Five

Black Consciousness and the Soweto Uprising

For opponents of apartheid, particularly young black South Africans, the 1970s were a decade of mounting frustration and anger. Also growing in the younger generation of South Africans was a new attitude of self-confidence, inspired by black activists and writers whose message was that freedom originated within the minds of individuals. Self-confidence sparked defiance, and unrest in the black townships gradually spread to the major cities.

The situation in the homelands was not improving. In 1970 the NP government passed the Bantu Homelands Act, which forced South Africa's blacks to become not just residents of self-governing, segregated territories, but citizens of the homeland, no longer citizens of South Africa. The homelands were made independent ministates, fractured islands without resources or power.

Ironically, the success of Verwoerd's Bantu education plan fueled unrest that followed. By the 1970s, the race-based school system had been in place for nearly twenty years. An entire generation of African students had been taught their "place" in South African society—a place, most realized, that afforded them no rights, no privileges, and almost no opportunities. In *South Africa: The Rise and Fall of Apartheid,* Nancy Clark and William Worger argue that "the sheer arrogance and brutality of apartheid made clear to all blacks that under this system they had no worth and no hope, and this left them with two choices: submit or rebel."[37]

Stephen Biko and Black Consciousness

In addition to learning that life under apartheid had little positive in store for them, the vast majority of black students were taught that they were inferior human beings whose highest aspiration was to become unskilled laborers.

Stephen Biko, a black college student studying to become a doctor at a nonwhite medical school, led a defiant response to those teachings. His philosophy of "black consciousness" emphasized self-esteem and rejected the idea that blacks were naturally inferior to whites and could never compete with whites economically or intellectually.

Biko also had a remarkably open definition of the word *black*. He argued that Indians, Africans, and people of mixed race should acknowledge a common identity as "black" people and work together to end apartheid. A dynamic journalist and personality, Biko was influenced by the civil rights movement in the United States and by the idea that being black was not a cause for shame. In his book *I Write What I Like,* Biko explained his notion of black consciousness:

Stephen Biko encouraged black South Africans to take pride in their racial identity.

> Black Consciousness is in essence the realization by the black man of the need to rally together with his brothers around the cause of their subjection—the blackness of their skin—and to operate as a group in order to rid themselves of the shackles that bind them to perpetual servitude. It seeks to demonstrate the lie that black is an aberration from the "normal" which is white. . . . It seeks to infuse the black community with a newfound pride in themselves, their efforts, their value systems, their culture, their religion and their outlook to life.[38]

While Biko was not antiwhite, his focus was black empowerment: He taught that freedom begins within each individual's mind and that Africans needed to liberate themselves first before throwing off the chains of others. As founder of the South African Students Organization (SASO), he organized a series of strikes and boycotts on university campuses in 1972. Two years later SASO angered the government by helping to organize rallies to celebrate the overthrow of white minority governments in the neighboring countries of Angola and Mozambique. The installation of black governments in those countries was a source of inspiration to South Africa's downtrodden blacks. The students who belonged to SASO believed that the same thing would happen in South Africa, and they said so on their banners and posters: "Change the name and the story applies to you. The dignity of the Black Man has been restored in Mozambique and so shall it be here. Black must rule. We shall drive them to the sea."[39]

Biko continued his activist activities despite four arrests as a revolutionary and conspirator between 1974 and 1977 and increasing restrictions imposed on his movements under antiterrorism laws. Many other SASO leaders and members were likewise arrested or "banned," and SASO itself was declared a banned organization in 1977. Like Mandela ten years earlier, Biko used his lengthy trial in 1974–75 as a forum to get his message out to fellow South Africans:

> I think the black man is subjected to two forces in this country. He is first of all oppressed . . . through laws that restrict him from doing certain things, through heavy work conditions, through poor pay, through very difficult living conditions, through poor education . . . and secondly, and this we regard as the most important, the black man . . . rejects himself, precisely because he attaches the meaning white to all that is good, in other words he associates good and he equates good with white.[40]

Biko and his codefendants were convicted of fomenting disorder and served various jail terms, but their convictions only seemed to strengthen the black consciousness movement.

Poverty, Despair, and Anger

Growing economic hardship during the 1970s gave Biko's words even greater impact. By 1973 the economy was in recession (reflecting a worldwide economic downturn connected with a crisis in oil production), leading to hundreds of strikes by black workers. Although black workers were crucial to the economy, the government did not treat them well. They were considered residents of their respective homelands and not true South Africans; therefore, the government felt no obligation to supply them with essential services. In the black townships where workers lived, little money was provided for hospitals, schools, electricity, or even running water.

In the overcrowded and desolate homelands, the situation was equally bleak for workers' families and the unemployed. The government had never provided the homelands with the resources to become economically independent. According to the government's own statistics, poverty levels in the homelands approached 80 percent by the end of the 1970s. The hopelessness and lack of job opportunities caused tens of thousands to leave. Desperate for work, they moved to the townships, even when they were breaking the law by doing so. In 1976, a typical four-room house in Soweto, a township outside Johannesburg, might have fifteen to twenty people living inside. Like the other townships, Soweto was essentially a giant labor barracks. Its sole function, as far as the government was concerned, was to provide white businesses with cheap labor.

As living conditions worsened for black South Africans, anger levels rose. In *The History of South Africa,* Roger Beck writes, "The pent-up rage and frustration that seethed throughout African townships by the mid-1970's created a powder keg that awaited a fuse."[41] The fuse was lit in Soweto. The spark was provided by the township's black schoolchildren.

In 1975 the white minister of Bantu education instructed all secondary schools that social studies and arithmetic must be taught in the Afrikaans language, an impossible demand that ensured that black students would receive an inferior education. Few black students or teachers spoke Afrikaans, and few would have used the despised language, identified as it was with the police and with apartheid, even if they could speak it. Parents, teachers, and students protested that the courses should be taught in English, the international language of business. The protests were ignored, even after Desmond Tutu, the Anglican bishop of Johannesburg, warned Prime Minister Vorster that violence was likely if the policy was not reversed.

The Soweto Uprising

On June 16, 1976, fifteen thousand Soweto schoolchildren marched to Orlando West Junior Secondary School. They carried signs ridiculing Afrikaans and calling on Vorster to learn Zulu. The demonstration was exuberant, marked by impassioned chants and upraised arms, but peaceful. But suddenly, the police shot tear gas into the crowd and then opened fire. Dozens were wounded, and at least two students were killed. A heart-wrenching photograph of a student carrying away the body of one of the victims, twelve-year-old Hector Petersen, was published in newspapers all over the world. What was called the Soweto massacre became an instant, international symbol of apartheid's brutality.

The South African government accepted no responsibility for the shootings. After the schools were shut down and the military put on full alert, Minister of Justice Jimmy Kruger accused the students of Communist allegiance. "Why do they walk with upraised fists?" he asked. "Surely this is the sign of the Communist Party."[42] Vowing that he would not be intimidated, Prime Minister Vorster told police and security forces to maintain order at all costs. The next day, angry riots broke out across much of the country, and at least 174 more Africans died. According to the official government figures (which were probably an underestimate), the violence that began in Soweto took 575 lives by the end of the year and wounded nearly 2,400 people. The students, however, were victorious in one sense: A month after the first protest, the government rescinded the instruction to teach the high school courses in Afrikaans.

Although the protests and rioting were undoubtedly influenced by the African National Congress (ANC), the Pan-Africanist Congress (PAC), and the black consciousness movement, they were not organized by any one individual or group. Instead, they were largely spontaneous

Stephen Biko's Gift

Archbishop Desmond Tutu explains the importance of martyred activist Stephen Biko to black South Africans:

I used to say that the Black Consciousness movement was surely of God. You see, the most awful aspect of oppression and injustice was not the untold suffering it visited on its victims and survivors, ghastly as that turned out to be. . . . No, it was the fact that apartheid could, through its treatment of God's children, actually make many of them doubt whether they were indeed God's children. That I have described as almost the ultimate blasphemy.

Black Consciousness sought to awaken in us the sense of our infinite value and worth in the sight of God because we were all created in God's image, so that our worth is intrinsic to who we are and not dependent on biological irrelevancies such as ethnicity, skin color or race. Black Consciousness helped to exorcise the horrible demons of self-hatred and self-contempt that made blacks suck up to whites whilst treating fellow blacks as the scum they thought themselves to be. . . .

How deeply indebted we are to Steve, acknowledged as the father of the Black Consciousness movement. We give thanks to God for him.

Desmond Tutu, preface to Stephen Biko, *I Write What I Like.* London: Bowerdean Press, 1996, pp. v, vi.

In 1977 mourners bear the coffin of Stephen Biko, who died of injuries sustained while in police custody, through the streets of King Williams Town.

Smoke billows from burning buildings on the streets of Soweto during rioting that followed the police shooting of peaceful protesters in June 1976.

reactions led by local student activists who paid a heavy price for their public stand. Those not killed outright were imprisoned by the hundreds. In most cases, their parents were not notified that their children had been arrested. Teenagers and even younger children died in police custody. Typically, the government would explain the deaths by claiming that the young prisoners had committed suicide, died while attempting to escape, or perished due to unknown causes.

The Murder of Biko

Evidence of government brutality in the aftermath of the Soweto uprising continued to inflame the situation. In the summer of 1977, the government issued a new warrant for the arrest of Stephen Biko, a man it regarded as exceptionally dangerous. Violating laws against distributing what the government called "inflammatory pamphlets,"[43] Biko had gone into hiding. Security police detained him at a roadblock near Grahamstown

A Student-Led Revolt

Students disgusted by what they considered the farce of Bantu education began the uprising in Soweto. According to the Illustrated History of South Africa: The Real Story, *the pig-headed insistence by authorities that classes be taught in Afrikaans was only the last straw:*

Of course, it was not so much Afrikaans as the whole system of Bantu education (and ultimately apartheid) that was the bone of contention for African students. This was apparent even before the outbreak of unrest. For instance, at the entrance of one Soweto school, pupils had daubed a slogan that read "Enter to learn, learn to serve." And during the protests a pamphlet addressed to parents stated ". . . you should rejoice for having given birth to this type of child . . . a child who prefers to die from a bullet rather than to swallow a poisonous education which relegates him and his parents to a position of perpetual subordination." On the same theme, a press statement released by the Soweto Students' Representative Council shortly after its formation in August 1976 stated: "Twenty years ago, when Bantu Education was introduced, our fathers said: 'Half a loaf is better than no loaf.' But we say: 'Half a gram of poison is just as killing as the whole gram.'"

Dougie Oakes, ed., *Illustrated History of South Africa: The Real Story*. Pleasantville, NY: Reader's Digest, 1989, p. 444.

On June 16, 1976, protesters in Soweto flee the scene after police open fire on what had been a peaceful demonstration.

on August 18. It was later revealed that he was kept naked and chained in a cell for the next twenty days. He was also severely beaten. Still in custody, he was then thrown naked into the back of a truck and driven seven hundred miles to Pretoria, where his death was announced on September 12.

The government claimed that Biko had died of brain damage suffered in a fall against a wall during a hunger strike. An official medical inquest concluded that his death was due to natural causes. But the government's official findings were condemned as outrageous around the world, and the ensuing outcry over Biko's death, almost certainly murder by official hands, further cemented South Africa's reputation for human rights abuses. That reputation was enhanced by comments like those of Minister of Justice Kruger, who said of Biko's death, "It leaves me cold."[44]

Biko had far less to do with the Soweto uprising than the government believed. It had in fact been started by schoolchildren who were then joined by workers. The stay-at-home strikes they organized were effective in further disrupting the country's economy. In the end, however, a lack of coordination and leadership allowed the uprising to die down. Eventually, the police regained control of the situation.

Apartheid on the Defensive

Still, the Soweto uprising was the most widespread outbreak of racial violence in South Africa's history. And, although the government reacted in its typical heavy-handed and brutal manner, the situation had fundamentally changed. In *A Traveller's History of South Africa,* David Mason argued that Soweto was the beginning of the end for apartheid:

> Although not many politicians and administrators could see it at the time, and even if they had would have been loath to admit it, apartheid was becoming less tenable with the passing of every year. In the aftermath of the Soweto uprising, it was on the brink of failing entirely. For this there were a number of reasons. On one level, governmental claims that normality had been restored after 1976–77 were a palpable untruth. Law and order may have been reimposed but the period of unrest had severely threatened the *status quo,* and as much as this situation had shaken many white people, it had given new hope and belief to African communities everywhere. As one commentator was to note later, the country's "psychic landscape had been transformed forever."[45]

Before Soweto, racial unrest in the country had been largely sporadic and contained. Apartheid seemed to be working for most white South Africans. Its supporters could, and did, claim that the policy was not only good for whites, it was doing what was best for blacks as well. They spoke of the South African government as a defender of democracy and justice. After the upris-

Who Were the Real Terrorists?

Bandile Mashinini's older brothers helped organize the Soweto uprising and then fled South Africa to avoid reprisals. Police harassed remaining family members in the aftermath of the uprising, as Mashinini explains to interviewer Tim McKee:

I remember one time I was playing outside and I saw three police vans pull up. I ran between the cops, and by the time I found my mom to tell her, four guns were pointed at both of our heads—rifles, shotguns, pistols, the works. Other times you'd hear noise outside, then boom, they were in the house, shaking you up on the bed. "Get up, *kaffir* [insulting term for a person of color], let's see who you are." They'd have this big flashlight in your face, guns pointing at you. . . .

Because my brothers were political, we had ANC T-shirts and documents in our house that in the eyes of the law were incriminating. We'd put them inside the coal stove and cover them up. But sometimes we'd sleep in those shirts, and a few nights when the cops came, it was like, "Wake up! Here's another terrorist wearing Mandela. In the van, buddy." They'd take people in my house to prison for a whole night's interrogation on why they were wearing a political T-shirt.

My mother was also arrested and spent seven months in solitary confinement. One of my brothers in exile tried to make contact with her, and somehow the police found out about it. The charge was aiding terrorists, helping them escape, which she did, but one has to ask—who were the terrorists really?

Quoted in Tim McKee, *No More Strangers Now: Young Voices from a New South Africa.* New York: Dorling Kindersley, 1998, pp. 66, 69.

ing in Soweto, the murder of Stephen Biko, and the disappearance of countless schoolchildren, those claims rang hollow—even to Afrikaners.

Other cracks in the structure of apartheid were becoming apparent. Since it relied so heavily on repression, including the exclusion of nonwhite leaders from the political process, the regime had cultivated no peaceful channels of communication with African, Indian, or Colored leaders to use when conflict arose. The only way it could respond to unrest was with guns, police, and security forces, a tactic guaranteed to increase resentment and worsen the situation.

It was also becoming clear to business leaders that maintaining the complete separation of the races was impossibly costly and economically counterproductive. Not only did South Africa's industries desperately need unskilled and skilled black workers, they needed to be confident that those workers would not be going on strike every few months. That was why the Federated Chambers of Commerce sent a letter to the prime minister asserting the need to have middle-class blacks "on our side."[46] The economic boom of the 1960s had turned into a recession in the 1970s. Repression, it was becoming clear, was not going to ensure prosperity and stability.

Meanwhile, South Africa had become an outcast among the world's nations. To protest its apartheid policy, many countries strictly limited trade with and investment in South Africa, which contributed to a decline of the whites' standard of living and a sense of foreboding among white Afrikaners, many of whom liquidated their assets and left the country. There was a growing realization among Afrikaner leaders that the apartheid envisioned by Hendrik Verwoerd—a country where nonwhites freely submitted to white domination and prospered in their segregated homelands—was an impossible dream.

Chapter Six

Battling the "Great Crocodile"

By 1978 Afrikaner leaders were beginning to realize that apartheid as it existed was unworkable. Although it was increasingly clear that without reforms the system would fall apart, most were reluctant to give up altogether on the idea of racial segregation and white dominance. Under the leadership of a new National Party (NP) prime minister, P.W. Botha, the government tinkered with the policy, attempting to put a kinder face on apartheid while ruthlessly stamping out all opposition. During Botha's tumultuous eleven-year rule, increasingly innovative strategies by the antiapartheid forces put Botha's regime on the defensive and brought South African society to the verge of collapse.

Even before becoming prime minister in 1978, Botha's pugnacious nature and violent temper had earned him the nickname the "Great Crocodile."[47] But despite his reputation as a hard-liner on apartheid, Botha surprised the world during his first years in office by proposing major reforms. Apartheid as it had been known, he said, would be ended: Afrikaners "must adapt or die."[48] Race relations would be restructured. Discrimination and injustice would be ended and restrictions on freedom of movement eased. Botha hoped this new policy would convince the world that South Africa was on an acceptably enlightened course.

A Suffering Economy

Botha was in fact bowing to pressure from South Africa's business community more than from the country's nonwhite majority or international detractors. When Botha took control of the country, business leaders demanded that he make major changes in apartheid. The social chaos—particularly the frequent strikes—was ruining them financially. And increasing threats of international boycotts made further economic woes likely. Disgust for apartheid had many countries considering more restrictions on their trade with South Africa. Further sanctions might destabilize not only the economy but the NP's hold on the government.

Botha agreed with business leaders that apartheid was a "recipe for permanent conflict."[49] Then, he shrewdly eased or discontinued those apartheid laws that were the most bothersome to enforce. The immorality and the mixed marriages acts, for example, were abolished, and official segregation of public places was ended. Although the pass laws remained in force—police retained the right to stop anyone at any time—enforcement was relaxed somewhat. By the early 1980s four of the black homelands had been granted nominal independence, official self-government that was mostly appeasement—their status was not recognized internationally—but, that many whites saw as a sign of things to come.

As whites began to consider the prospect of black rule and perhaps black backlash against the white minority—a real possibility—white emigration increased,

Under pressure from South Africa's business community, Prime Minister P. W. Botha eased some of the harshest aspects of apartheid.

and South African industry faced shortages of skilled workers and managers. The country needed educated blacks to run its mines and factories. Botha, therefore, agreed to ease the laws prohibiting nonwhites from working in skilled jobs.

At the request of white business leaders, Botha also legalized black trade unions. The hope was that, if management had someone to negotiate with, costly strikes could be averted. The move, however, had far-reaching and unforeseen consequences in the battle to end apartheid. In the absence of any other legal avenues of communication, black trade unions became powerful political representatives of the people. Throughout the 1980s, South Africa's nonwhite majority frequently expressed its dissatisfaction with apartheid through trade union officials.

Protests were frequent because the government had no plans to significantly relinquish white South Africans' political dominance. Botha remained determined to weaken any African opposition. The relatively cosmetic changes in apartheid he made were designed to stabilize the economy while defusing the main grievances of nonwhites. In *The History of South Africa,* Roger Beck describes the underlying motives of the National Party: "They told the world that South Africa had changed, even that apartheid was dead; but White, particularly Afrikaner control over a White South Africa remained their goal."[50]

Total Strategy

The changes in apartheid were part of a new policy called Total Strategy. The aim of Total Strategy was to boost South Africa's public image, maintain apartheid in some less offensive form, and strengthen national (that is, white) security. Security was a huge concern of the National Party and of almost all Afrikaners, who believed that apartheid was essential to their very survival as a people. Not only did they fear that the nonwhite majority would rise up and overthrow them, they were also convinced that Marxist revolutionaries elsewhere in Africa, sponsored by the Soviet Union, were working to overthrow the South African regime and set up a Communist puppet state. Total Strategy was seen as a way to battle the perceived Communist threat.

These fears were not unfounded. By the 1980s, amid an era of nationalist and anticolonial movements across Africa, most of South Africa's neighbors had new governments in which the native peoples who were in the majority had full representation. The rulers of these countries were sympathetic to the political demands of South Africa's nonwhites. Well aware that revolutionary movements in nearby countries threatened apartheid, Botha ordered South African military and security forces to conduct secret operations in countries like Mozambique and Zimbabwe. The aim was to destabilize governments that could provide support to the enemies of apartheid. The military also operated more openly in Namibia and even engaged in a full-scale war in Angola.

South African military forces also battled homegrown enemies of apartheid such as the African National Congress

Death at the Door

Antiapartheid clergyman Allan Boesak was a leader of South Africa's black theology movement, which holds that Christianity supports the struggle and liberation of the poor from oppression (in some interpretations, so-called liberation theology condones violence as a means to that end). An interview with Jim Wallis for the book Crucible of Fire: The Church Confronts Apartheid *hints at the kind of courage and commitment it took to publicly oppose apartheid:*

Years ago I had an experience. This white man came to my door, and he said, "I have been in prayer and fasting for a week or two now. God told me about what a danger you are to this country. He also told me that you would have to die and I would be your executioner if you don't stop this."

That was the first time I had been faced physically with something like that. I remember just standing there trembling. I didn't even say anything back to him. I just closed the door and leaned against it. And my son Allan, then two years old, came running up the passage. As I hugged him, I understood for the first time, I think, what I was doing to my family.

I was completely shaken up. And I found that I had to pray out loud. I couldn't just say the words in my heart, because I was afraid that if I didn't hear the words, I wouldn't be able to keep them. . . .

Now death squads are something that we've become used to. Friends have been murdered quite cold-bloodedly. I said to the church, "You ought to know there have been threats. You ought to know also that I'm not a particularly brave person. But I do feel that what we're doing is the call of the gospel."

Jim Wallis and Joyce Hollyday, *Crucible of Fire: The Church Confronts Apartheid.* Washington, DC: Orbis, 1989, pp. 52–53.

(ANC), whose military wing, Spear of the Nation, had regrouped in the late 1970s and was conducting guerrilla warfare. From bases and training camps in Angola and Mozambique, Spear of the Nation fighters returned to South Africa to set off car bombs and sabotage power plants. Meanwhile, South African security forces operated secretly in a half dozen countries. They indiscriminately kidnapped, tortured, and executed thousands of Africans of all races suspected of opposing apartheid.

When members of the security forces finished their tour of duty and returned home to South Africa, they brought the same brutal tactics with them. During the 1980s, political killings and disappearances increased inside South Africa. The rise in government killings highlighted the contradictions of Total Strategy. In effect, it was a policy that was working against itself—it tried to be both harsher and softer at the same time. The contradictions eventually led to its total collapse.

The Constitution Fiasco

Arguably, Total Strategy's biggest failure was the attempt to change South Africa's constitution. The rewriting of the constitution was part of a new series of reforms introduced in 1984 in the hope they would reduce internal opposition to apartheid. Botha proposed that the parliament be split into three separate chambers, one for Whites, one for Coloreds, and one for Asians. Although each racial group would have responsibility for its schools, hospitals, and community affairs, a white president would retain overall control of all three chambers. Africans, meanwhile, would be denied any role because, according to the government, they already had voting rights in their homelands. They were, however, granted more local control over the townships, yet they were still forbidden to live and work where they wanted.

The new constitution was meant to show that the government sincerely wanted to share power. The real intent, however, was to split antiapartheid opposition, thereby maintaining white dominance. The reforms, according to Peter Ackerman and Jack Duvall, authors of *A Force More Powerful*, "rearranged the furniture of apartheid without changing the floor plan of white power."[51] Although white voters approved the changes in a referendum, nonwhite Africans were not fooled by the scheme. While speaking at a conference in Johannesburg, a Colored minister named Allan Boesak, president of the World Alliance of Reformed Churches, proposed that a new national opposition should be formed to boycott the elections. He suggested that it should be composed of trade unions, churches, civic groups, and student organizations. According to Ackerman and Duvall, Boesak's idea met with an enthusiastic response:

> On August 20, 1983, people from more than 500 organizations rallied in a community center in Mitchells Plain, a Colored township outside Cape Town to launch the United Democratic Front (UDF). The hall was so packed that some people hung from the rafters; others listened from under a tent pitched nearby, while more sat outside as light rain fell. The delegates—Whites, Coloreds, Africans and Indians—included veterans of ANC campaigns in the 1950s and young people who had watched as police shot down their schoolmates on Soweto's streets in 1976. Civics[sic], churches, women, students, and labor unions were represented. The new group's structure was decentralized, but it had a single goal, and Allan Boesak made no bones about what it was: "We want all our rights, and we want them here and we want them now."[52]

Intended to bolster white rule, Botha's proposed constitutional changes had instead united the majority of South Africans against the government. As a multiracial organization, the UDF welcomed anyone willing to join. It was dedicated to representing the ANC and the democratic principles that had been proclaimed nearly thirty years before in the Freedom Charter. It advocated nonviolent opposition to apartheid primarily through the use of boycotts. By 1984 the UDF had the support of some six hundred organizations and some 3 million people of all races.

Change and Violence

It was as if the "wind of change" that Harold Macmillan had spoken about in 1960 was finally blowing across the nation. Even white South Africans were publicly expressing doubts about apartheid. The largest Afrikaner church had long been a champion of apartheid. But in April 1984 the Western Synod of the Dutch Reformed Church shocked its members by urging them to confess their participation in apartheid with sorrow and humility: "There is no such thing as white superiority or black inferiority. . . . All people are equal before God. . . . There may not be

As president of the World Alliance of Reformed Churches, Allan Boesak encouraged nonwhite South Africans to boycott the referendum on a new national constitution.

Following rioting in black townships in August 1985, South African military forces were called in to restore order.

under any circumstances a political policy based on oppression, discrimination and exploitation. . . . The task of the Church is to protest against unjust laws."[53] Such sentiments, however, were not common among white South Africans.

Throughout 1984 and 1985 the level of resistance to apartheid rose. The UDF sponsored boycotts and organized campaigns in which township residents withheld their rent to protest against high charges for electricity and water. In the spring of 1985 the ANC called for people to "Make apartheid unworkable! Make the country ungovernable!"[54] Stay-at-homes from schools and workplaces became more and more common. The reaction of the police and security forces—relying on violence and detention without charge—only worsened the situation. In some parts of the country a state of virtual civil war existed.

The violence was not just between police and protesters. Black-on-black violence emerged as a significant, and tragic, problem at this time. Militant groups of blacks, mostly students and young adults, formed makeshift courts that tried men and women suspected of being informers or collaborating with white authorities. If a person was found guilty, a rubber tire filled with gasoline was placed around his or her neck and lit on fire. As Beck notes, this cruel method of execution was called "necklacing."[55] Hundreds were killed in this fashion as gruesome images of the victims appeared on television screens all over the world. Desmond Tutu, the Anglican bishop of Johannesburg who was awarded the Nobel Peace Prize in 1985 for his principled opposition to apartheid, was so sickened by the killing of a twelve-year-old girl suspected of being an informer that he threatened to move away from South Africa if such barbarism continued.

Although Botha relaxed the pass laws in 1985, violence and bloodshed continued. When riots erupted after police shot and killed twenty demonstrators commemorating the Sharpeville atrocities, Botha declared a state of emergency. The army was sent into the townships to restore order, and censorship was tightened so images of the violence would not reach the outside world. Despite this clampdown on information, international condemnation of South Africa reached an all-time high.

New Negotiations with the ANC

As the situation continued to deteriorate, a desperate Botha turned to Nelson Mandela, still the antiapartheid movement's

An Economy with No Future

A change in international banking policy in 1985 left South Africa's white minority strapped for investment cash, greatly hastening the end of apartheid, according to historian Brian Lapping:

Since 1960, anti-apartheid movements worldwide had been demanding that big companies and banks stop investing in South Africa. The demand had little effect. In 1985, however, the big international banks changed sides. For decades they had insisted that they looked only at balance sheets, that if they worried about the human rights or social policies of governments they would have to withdraw from half the world. But in 1985 the large New York bank, Chase Manhattan, influenced by students, churches and charities that had withdrawn deposits rather than have them invested in South Africa, refused to renew a major South African loan. Other banks quickly followed suit. Suddenly respectable bankers, long committed to avoiding meddling in politics, decided that here things were different. Together they informed the South African Finance Minister . . . that future loans would be forthcoming only if South Africa settled its internal political problems.

Brian Lapping, *Apartheid: A History*. New York: George Braziller, 1987, p. 181.

unquestioned moral leader after twenty years in prison and perhaps the only person whose call to quell the violence might be heeded. Botha promised he would free Mandela if the ANC would renounce the use of violence as a political instrument. Suspecting Botha's motives, Mandela refused the offer. Had he agreed to it, the government could blame any future outbreaks of violence on the ANC. Mandela's response, his first public words in twenty years, was read by his daughter Zinzi to cheers and applause at a UDF rally in Soweto:

> I cherish my own freedom dearly, but I care even more for your freedom. Too many have died since I went to prison. Too many have suffered for the love of freedom. I owe it to their widows, to their orphans, to their mothers and to their fathers who have grieved and wept for them. . . . I am not less life-loving than you are. But I cannot sell my birthright, nor am I prepared to sell the birthright of the people to be free. I am in prison as the representative of the people and of your organization, the African National Congress, which was banned.
>
> What freedom am I being offered while the organization of the people remains banned? What freedom am I being offered when I may be arrested on a pass offense? What freedom am I being offered to live my life as a family with my dear wife who remains in banishment in Brandfort? What freedom am I being offered when I need a stamp in my pass to seek work? What freedom am I being offered when my very South African citizenship is not respected?
>
> Only free men can negotiate. Prisoners cannot enter into contracts. . . . I cannot and will not give any undertaking at a time when I and you, the people, are not free.[56]

Foreign governments increasingly decided to acknowledge the ANC as the legitimate representative of South Africa's blacks and to pressure Botha's government to open formal negotiations with the ANC. When the government refused to do so, white South African business and religious leaders flew to Zambia and met with Oliver Tambo, the ANC's president-in-exile. Although Tambo and his organization were considered "terrorist murderers"[57] by the South African government, the meetings continued throughout 1985 and 1986. The ANC's prestige and popularity was further enhanced in 1987 when U.S. officials met with Tambo.

Negotiations acquired a special urgency because international sanctions and social unrest were crippling South Africa's economy. The withdrawal of foreign investments helped cause a collapse in the value of South Africa's currency. The Johannesburg Stock Exchange even had to close for a while as more and more nations severed their economic ties with South Africa. Although struggling South African business leaders pleaded with Botha to relax or end apartheid, he did neither.

Obstinate to the End

Abandoning further attempts at reform, the government rejected all suggestions that the system should be changed. Instead, it clamped down hard, pouring money, personnel, and equipment into enforcing security. Under the declared state of emergency, the police were given the power to arrest and imprison virtually anyone—whether suspected of a crime or not. Army troops were deployed alongside the police in townships and homelands. In addition, paramilitary forces arrested, detained, and sometimes secretly executed suspected antiapartheid activists. Many arrestees were abused or tortured; children as young as ten were subjected to electric shock during interrogations. In addition, the government looked the other way when white vigilante groups struck against apartheid opponents.

Although lawlessness and violence permeated South African society, security forces reestablished a fragile order by the beginning of 1988. Soldiers, police, and paramilitary security forces, with their machine guns and armored cars, were deployed in townships all over the nation. The uneasy calm they enforced was bought at the expense of hundreds of black lives. Thousands more blacks languished behind bars. At a time when the South African economy was in crisis, the white power structure was funding an enormously costly military operation with no end in sight.

With the black population essentially locked down, apartheid had reached a dead end. The government did not have the resources to hold down political unrest indefinitely. On the other hand, antiapartheid forces did not have the strength to sweep the government from power. The political situation was deadlocked, but it would not stay that way for long.

Chapter Seven

The End of Apartheid

In 1989 prime minister P.W. Botha resigned in a fit of anger over criticism by his own party. His resignation marked the beginning of one of the most remarkable periods of transformation any nation has ever undergone. Under the enlightened leadership of men like Nelson Mandela, Bishop Desmond Tutu, and the new prime minister, F.W. de Klerk, the rigid structures of apartheid collapsed. Despite predictions of catastrophe, the country did not descend into civil war. The next few years would be tumultuous and violent, but in the end South Africa would succeed in making the transition to democratic rule, an achievement hailed around the world.

F.W. de Klerk was an unlikely figure to be at the center of such momentous change. An unremarkable cabinet minister since 1978, he assumed power in September 1989. De Klerk's record suggested that he would continue Botha's policies. But unlike hard-core apartheid backers, de Klerk was a pragmatist. No one could deny that, despite soldiers, guns, prisons, and police, more and more civilians were defying the government. Along with a growing number of business and government leaders, de Klerk concluded that South African society was headed for collapse. "The impracticability, unacceptability and unaffordability of apartheid" he said, "meant that the whole system is falling apart . . . the black revolt is becoming uncontrollable."[58]

A Turning Point

Many Afrikaners wanted to believe that apartheid could be modified in some way to reduce black dissatisfaction yet maintain white dominance. Those on the front lines of the battle, men like provincial chief of police intelligence Lourence DuPlessis, disagreed. They realized that a turning point had been reached. "[Black South Africans] just didn't want apartheid anymore," said DuPlessis. "That's what it

In 2004 Archbishop Desmond Tutu (left) speaks with the two men most responsible for bringing an end to apartheid, F. W. de Klerk and Nelson Mandela.

boils down to. They were not prepared to be suppressed any longer."[59]

During de Klerk's first two months in office he was greeted by a massive campaign of civil disobedience. It was organized by the Mass Democratic Movement (MDM), successor to the United Democratic Front (UDF), which had been banned by Botha. Peaceful marches were held in every major town and city in the country. But this time de Klerk instructed the security forces to let the demonstrations run their course. His decision was one of the first indications that government policy had changed.

Soon after that, de Klerk began releasing political prisoners. Then, in December, he met with Mandela in prison. According to Peter Ackerman and Jack Duvall, authors of *A Force More Power-*

ful, de Klerk had concluded that the government's position would become weaker the longer it waited to deal with apartheid. "Moreover, if he waited too long, he might lose the opportunity to deal with Mandela and the older generation of [African National Congress] ANC leaders who seemed to be more conciliatory than their junior associates."[60]

On February 2, 1990, during the opening session of parliament, de Klerk stunned the world by announcing that he was willing and ready to negotiate with antiapartheid leaders:

> The alternative is growing violence, tension and conflict. That is unacceptable and in nobody's interest. The well-being of all in this country is linked inextricably to the ability of the leaders to come to terms with one another. . . . No one can escape this simple truth.
>
> On its part, the Government will accord the process of negotiation the highest priority. The aim is a total new and just constitutional dispensation in which every inhabitant will enjoy equal rights, treatment and opportunity.[61]

De Klerk followed that bombshell by announcing that he was lifting the ban on the ANC, the Pan-Africanist Congress (PAC), the UDF, and thirty other organizations.

Mandela Freed

Nine days later, Nelson Mandela was released after 27 years in prison. The actual release was a historic event, covered by the world's news agencies. As historian Roger Beck notes, "In the space of a few feet Mandela went from being a prisoner to being a statesman of international stature."[62] In bright sunshine the elderly, dignified Mandela, now seventy-one years old, walked in a procession through cheering crowds to the town hall in Cape Town. From its balcony he addressed the huge crowd, many of whom were glimpsing their famous leader for the first time. Millions more around the world watched the extraordinary drama live on television.

Some observers worried that Mandela might have been forced to compromise his principles in order to win release from prison. Any doubts were extinguished, however, when he raised his fist and shouted, *"Amandla!"*—the Zulu word for "power." A tremendous roar came from the crowd as they recognized the beginning of the chant that had long been an anthem of the black resistance movement. After thanking everyone who had worked for his freedom for so long, Mandela told the crowd, "Your tireless and heroic sacrifices have made it possible for me to be here today. I therefore place the remaining years of my life in your hands."[63]

Although the mood was triumphant, Mandela emphasized that the battle against apartheid was not over:

> Our struggle has reached a decisive moment. We call on our people to seize this moment so that the process towards democracy is rapid and uninterrupted. We have waited too

> long for our freedom. We can no longer wait. Now is the time to intensify the struggle on all fronts. To relax our efforts now would be a mistake which generations to come will not be able to forgive. The sight of freedom looming on the horizon should encourage us to redouble our efforts.
>
> It is only through disciplined mass action that our victory can be assured. We call on our white compatriots to join us in the shaping of a new South Africa. The freedom movement is a political home for you too. We call on the international community to continue the campaign to isolate the apartheid regime. To lift sanctions now would be to run the risk of aborting the process towards the complete eradication of apartheid. Our march to freedom is irreversible. We must not allow fear to stand in our way.[64]

Mandela ended his speech by reaffirming, as he had at his trial in 1964, that he was ready to die for his vision of a free, peaceful, and harmonious society.

De Klerk's Aims

De Klerk, too, claimed to be working toward a society where all people were equal, but he had entrenched interests to protect. Although he had loosened the reins of apartheid because he believed the economy would collapse if he did not, his main concern was keeping the National Party (NP) in power. In the most recent elections, the NP had lost votes to the Conservative Party (CP), a group that remained staunchly in favor of apartheid. CP leaders claimed that Botha and de Klerk had already granted nonwhites too much power. Their solution to South Africa's problems was to enforce segregation more strictly. The CP's stance was attracting fearful white voters and weakening the NP.

De Klerk's ultimate goal was to retain NP control over as much of the government as possible. He hoped that the concessions made to nonwhites would improve economic conditions enough to cause white voters who had deserted the NP to return to his party. He also believed that it would take the ANC a while to adjust to its new legal status. In the meantime, he was confident he could outmaneuver its leaders politically.

A New Cycle of Violence

Despite the sense that reform was finally at hand, the violence did not abate. In March, only two days before talks between the ANC and de Klerk's government were scheduled to begin, police and armed white civilians fired on a march of fifty thousand ANC supporters near Johannesburg. Eleven people were killed and more than four hundred were injured in the township of Sebokeng. The massacre marked the beginning of a campaign of shooting and bombing that would last for the next four years and take between fourteen thousand and fifteen thousand lives. White supremacist groups, often working with security forces, targeted members of the ANC, publishers of antiapartheid news-

A Surge of Joy

In his autobiography, Mandela describes his reactions to the reception he faced as he walked out of prison a free man on February 11, 1990. He had expected no more than a few dozen people—not thousands of well-wishers.

Within twenty feet or so of the gate, the cameras started clicking, a noise that sounded like some great herd of metallic beasts. Reporters started shouting questions; television crews began crowding in; ANC supporters were yelling and cheering. It was a happy, if slightly disorienting chaos. When a television crew thrust a long, dark, furry object at me, I recoiled slightly, wondering if it were some newfangled weapon developed while I was in prison. [Mandela's wife] Winnie informed me that it was a microphone.

When I was among the crowd I raised my right fist and there was a roar. I had not been able to do that for twenty-seven years and it gave me a surge of strength and joy. We stayed among the crowd for only a few minutes before jumping back into the car for the drive to Cape Town. Although I was pleased to have such a reception, I was greatly vexed by the fact that I did not have a chance to say good-bye to the prison staff. As I finally walked through those gates to enter a car on the other side, I felt—even at the age of seventy-one—that my life was beginning anew. My ten thousand days of imprisonment were over.

Nelson Mandela, *Long Walk to Freedom: The Autobiography of Nelson Mandela.* Boston: Little, Brown, 1994, pp. 490–91.

Shortly after his release from prison, Nelson Mandela raises his fist in the air, symbolizing the triumph of black South Africans over apartheid.

papers, and people of all races and religions who advocated the end of apartheid. By the end of the year the number of murders caused by political violence was averaging one hundred a month.

Not all of the violence was white against black. In parts of South Africa virtual civil war broke out between the ANC/UDF forces and the influential rival Inkatha organization. Inkatha had been founded in 1975 to preserve Zulu culture. Its name is taken from the grass coil used to bear loads on the head, a symbol of the Zulus. Its leader, Mangosotho Buthelezi, was a Zulu chief and leader of the Zulus' homeland. Buthelezi had been a member of the ANC Youth League. Inkatha emerged in the vacuum left by the banning of the ANC as an important black political organization, but one significant difference—Inkatha refused to advocate armed struggle against white rule—led to deep division and bitterness between the groups and ultimately fighting among blacks. In 1990 Buthelezi formed a national political party, the Inkatha Freedom Party (IFP), committed to nonviolent, democratic reforms.

In the IFP, de Klerk and the NP saw an opportunity to split the black vote and diminish the power of the ANC. As violence escalated between the two organizations, it was revealed that the government was secretly funding the IFP. At that point, Mandela lost his trust in de Klerk. Earlier, de Klerk had rejected Mandela's idea that South Africa should become a true democracy, stating that "majority rule

All Men Are Capable of Change

During his twenty-seven years in prison Mandela always behaved civilly to his guards because he believed that hostility was self-defeating. Still, he was taken aback when Piet Badenhorst, a notoriously brutal prison officer who was about to be transferred, called Mandela into his office and wished him good luck.

I thought about this moment for a long time afterward. Badenhorst had perhaps been the most callous and barbaric commanding officer we had had on Robben Island. But that day in the office he had revealed that there was another side to his nature, a side that had been obscured but that still existed. It was a useful reminder that all men, even the most seemingly cold-blooded, have a core of decency, and that if their heart is touched, they are capable of changing.

Nelson Mandela, *Long Walk to Freedom: The Autobiography of Nelson Mandela.* Boston: Little, Brown, 1994, pp. 402–403.

on the basis of one man, one vote was not suitable for a country such as South Africa because it leads to domination and even suppression of minorities."[65] By "minorities" de Klerk clearly meant white people. Power sharing, as far as the NP was concerned, was not going to mean majority rule.

Mandela Versus de Klerk

De Klerk, however, did proceed with reforms reducing white social privilege. By early 1991 laws concerning land ownership, segregation, and the use of racial categories were repealed. These reforms, de Klerk believed, put him in a position to control the outcome when he met with Mandela and representatives of the ANC and twenty other political organizations in the fall of 1991. The Convention for a Democratic South Africa (CODESA) was called in order to begin talks on how the country would be transformed. The talks got off to a rocky start with an angry exchange between Mandela and de Klerk. Little was accomplished in the first few months, but that lack of progress was acceptable to the whites, who feared any change in their status.

As 1992 began, de Klerk's administration remained in full control of the state. Most Afrikaners assumed he would be able to manipulate the negotiations to prevent majority rule. Nelson Mandela, however, was a more formidable political opponent than any de Klerk had ever faced. His goal was to transform the government from one based on the principle of "divide and rule" to one based on true democratic principles.

The aftermath of two pivotal events in 1992 greatly weakened de Klerk and set the stage for Mandela's triumph. The first came on the night of June 17 when a group of Inkatha supporters infiltrated Vaal township and murdered forty-six people, mostly women and children. White security forces did nothing to prevent the massacre and afterward showed no interest in finding the guilty parties. Enraged by the government's inaction—"Mr. De Klerk said nothing. I found this to be the last straw and my patience snapped"[66]—Mandela broke off negotiations with the government and called for mass action. That August he led one hundred thousand supporters on a march to the headquarters of government in Pretoria. At the same time, a two-day general strike brought the nation to an economic standstill.

The second pivotal event was the massacre of twenty-nine ANC supporters on September 7, when soldiers fired into a crowd of some seventy thousand ANC marchers in the Ciskei homeland. The soldiers were under the command of Brigadier Oupa Gqoza, the homeland's leader. Like the leader of the Zulu homeland, Gqoza viewed true democracy as a threat to his own power. Suspecting that Gqoza had acted at the urging of the government, Mandela accused de Klerk of being responsible for the killings. Although de Klerk denied involvement, ample evidence surfaced that security forces were participating in the political killings ravaging the nation. When a government commission of inquiry uncovered plans by military intelligence to

Nelson Mandela and F. W. de Klerk proudly display their Nobel Peace Prize medals following the presentation ceremony in Oslo, Norway, in December 1993.

destabilize the ANC, de Klerk's credibility was damaged even further.

Pulling Back from the Brink

With the CODESA talks suspended and relations between Mandela and de Klerk frosty, it seemed as if the nation was headed for civil war. At that point the two men began acting like true statesmen. As Frank Welsh noted in his history of South Africa, "the bloody events that followed the failure [to continue talking] shocked the leaders on both sides into a realization that they must act together to prevent the complete disintegration of South African society."[67]

Three weeks after the massacre in Ciskei, the two men signed an agreement to resume negotiations in April 1993. Meanwhile, secret talks between the ANC and the government produced a new sense of trust. The momentum for change increased as European countries, then the United States, lifted economic sanctions. In October, Mandela and de Klerk were jointly awarded the Nobel Peace Prize. A few weeks later a new constitution was approved—one that gave equal voting rights to every South African regardless of race. The date set for the country's first multiracial election was April 27, 1994.

Extremist groups worked hard to disrupt the election. White extremists continued their bombings and killings, and Inkatha supporters so strongly opposed the new constitution that the government had to declare a state of emergency in the province of Natal. Despite the background of turmoil, the elections went off peacefully and, for the most part, joyfully. Some 19.7 million voters went to the polls, an amazing 86 percent of eligible voters. They were presented with a choice of candidates from nearly twenty political parties, running for seats in the National Assembly and provin-

A New Beginning

Leandra Jansen van Vuuren, a fifteen-year-old Afrikaner farm girl, was raised to believe that blacks were dangerous and inferior, but her attitude began to change after she went to a camp with children of all races. Two years after Nelson Mandela was elected president, van Vuuren described her response to the admission of black students to her school:

Most of the kids at school don't know what I've learned. If a black girl comes close, a lot of them will just move away. I can see that they are afraid to mix; I know this because I was afraid, too. But I've made a new beginning, and I think it's important now to try and change things at my school. The message I want to give is that everyone must learn to respect one another and that will make life far easier. Apartheid gave us a very bad image of the blacks; it didn't tell us the truth. That is what we have to change, so that we see them as they really are, not what we think they are. If we don't respect them, we won't ever have a day when we say, "We're sorry, we were blind."

Quoted in Tim McKee, *No More Strangers: Young Voices from a New South Africa.* New York: Dorling Kindersley, 1998, p. 17.

cial legislatures. Perhaps the most dramatic race was for the presidency—Mandela versus de Klerk, the two most prominent symbols of the end of apartheid.

The First Free Election

Black South Africans did not take the responsibility lightly: Most were voting for the first time in their lives. Despite long lines, they waited to cast their ballots with dignity and patience. In his biography of Mandela, Martin Meredith noted that the experience was often just as powerful for whites:

> For many whites, the experience of the election was as moving as it was for blacks. Standing side by side with blacks, waiting to vote, they felt a sense of their own liberation. The feelings of relief that the curse of apartheid had finally been lifted were

Thousands of supporters raise their fists to salute Nelson Mandela as he is inaugurated as South Africa's first black president in 1994.

Calming a Country

During Nelson Mandela's campaign for president he delivered messages aimed at diminishing both unrealistic fears and unrealistic expectations. This approach, as Mandela explains, helped calm the nation.

Just as we told the people what we would do, I felt we must also tell them what we could not do. Many people felt life would change overnight after a free and democratic election, but that would be far from the case. Often, I said to crowds, "Do not expect to be driving a Mercedes the day after the election or swimming in your own backyard pool." I told supporters, "Life will not change dramatically, except that you will have increased your self-esteem and become a citizen in your own land. You must have patience. You might have to wait five years for results to show." I challenged them; I did not patronize them: "If you want to continue living in poverty without clothes and food," I told them, "then go and drink in the shebeens [taverns]. But if you want better things, you must work hard. We cannot do it all for you; you must do it yourselves."

I told white audiences that we needed them and did not want them to leave the country. They were South Africans just like ourselves and this was their land, too. I would not mince words about the horrors of apartheid, but I said, over and over, that we should forget the past and concentrate on building a better future for all.

Nelson Mandela, *Long Walk to Freedom: The Autobiography of Nelson Mandela.* Boston: Little, Brown, 1994, p. 535.

as strong among the white community which had imposed it as among the blacks who suffered under it.[68]

The outcome, according to Martin Meredith, was never in doubt because so many millions of South Africans identified with Mandela:

His ordeal of imprisonment had never been forgotten by the people for whom he spoke and was duly acknowledged when the time came for them to vote. Time and again, it was said, "He went to prison for us." For blacks, the election was, above all, about liberation—a celebration of their freedom from white rule—and it was to Mandela's leadership that many attributed that liberation.[69]

As his daughter Zenani looks on, Nelson Mandela congratulates F. W. de Klerk after he is sworn in as deputy vice president.

As expected, Mandela and the ANC won by a landslide, receiving 62 percent of the vote and 252 seats in the National Assembly. The NP attracted enough votes—20.4 percent and 82 seats—to ensure that de Klerk would serve as one of Mandela's two deputy vice presidents. Inkatha was the third-highest vote getter, with 10.5 percent of the vote and 43 seats. Gracious in defeat, de Klerk offered "congratulations, good wishes and prayers" and said, "I hold out my hand to Mr. Mandela in friendship and in cooperation."[70]

Celebrating a New President

On Mandela's inauguration day, May 10, 1994, the country threw the biggest celebration in its history. Four thousand dignitaries from all over the world attended the ceremony. The seventy-five-year-old former prisoner's eloquence matched the occasion:

> Out of the experience of an extraordinary human disaster that lasted too long must be born a society of which all humanity will be proud. . . . We have triumphed in the effort to implant hope in the breasts of the millions of our people. We enter into a covenant that we shall build the society in which all South Africans, both black and white, will be able to walk tall, without any fear in their hearts, assured of their inalienable right to human dignity—a rainbow nation at peace with itself and the world.[71]

At one point the crowd arose spontaneously to cheer and applaud. Mandela's stirring words that pulled them from their seats made it clear that, finally, the nightmare of apartheid was over:

> Never, never and never again shall it be that this beautiful land will again experience the oppression of one by another, and suffer the indignity of being the skunk of the world. Let freedom reign![72]

Epilogue

Truth and Reconciliation

Despite Mandela's election to the presidency, most South Africans realized that the dark shadow of apartheid still hung over the nation. Bitterness over the brutal crimes committed during the apartheid era ran deep. Unless the country found a way to heal those wounds, they would, in the words of Nelson Mandela, "live with us like a festering sore."[73]

National healing was the idea behind the creation of the Truth and Reconciliation Commission in 1995. Known as the truth commission, this courtlike body was headed by Nobel Peace Prize winner Archbishop Desmond Tutu. Its purpose was to assemble as complete a picture as possible of the human rights abuses carried out between 1960 and 1994. Only through full disclosure, it was thought, could South Africa move beyond its shameful past. The truth commission, which began two years of hearings in April 1996, was a model of democracy. All South Africans who felt they had been a victim of violence could sign up to give testimony. During the commission's three years of existence, more than twenty-two thousand people did so. Many of them were awarded reparations for what their government had done to them.

Their stories were both gripping and horrifying. Victims described how they were imprisoned without trial and then raped and tortured so violently that survivors were routinely left blind or crippled. During the 1970s and '80s the government conducted most of its operations against suspected anti-apartheid activists in secret. For millions—both black and white—the graphic testimony before the truth commission, much of it televised, exposed the true nature of apartheid for the first time.

The Value of Truth

The most controversial aspect of the truth commission's work was its granting of amnesty. Archbishop Tutu and others realized that perpetrators of human rights violations knew many dark secrets. Unless a way was found to get them to talk, what had happened to thousands of victims might never be known. Tutu firmly believed that only after the truth was acknowledged could the victims of apartheid—and the nation itself—move forward.

Therefore, perpetrators of crimes under apartheid were granted immunity from prosecution if the commission concluded that they had provided honest public testimony about their abuses. It was the only way that families of victims—and the nation—could learn what had really happened to the thousands of people who, after being taken into custody, had simply vanished. Thanks to

This corridor in Robben Island prison, which today houses a museum, is where Nelson Mandela was confined for twenty-seven years.

Acknowledging Truth, Seeking Reconciliation

The testimony before the Truth and Reconciliation Commission was so heart-wrenching that on the second day of hearings Archbishop Tutu laid his head down on a table and wept. Painful as the process was, victims reported being gratified by abusers' public admission of their acts. Chronicler Martin Meredith quotes a typical exchange between a police officer named Jeffrey Benzien and a captured insurgent named Peter Jacobs.

JACOBS: So, you would undress me, tie my blue belt around my feet, throw me on the ground, put the handcuffs with the cloth over my arm to prevent marks. You do that [give electric shocks] quite a few times. But at some point, I think it is about the fourth time, when I thought I am dying, you woke me up and said, "Peter, I will take you to the verge of death as many times as I want to. But you are going to talk and if it means you will die, that is okay." Do you remember that?

BENZIEN: I concede I may have said that, Sir.

JACOBS: I want you to tell me, because this is important for me. The truth commission can [grant] amnesty, but this is important for me. Did you say that?

BENZIEN: Yes, I did say that.

Quoted in Martin Meredith, *Coming to Terms: South Africa's Search for Truth.* New York: PublicAffairs, 1999, pp. 131–32.

In a gesture of reconciliation, a white and a black South African clasp hands in this 1995 photo.

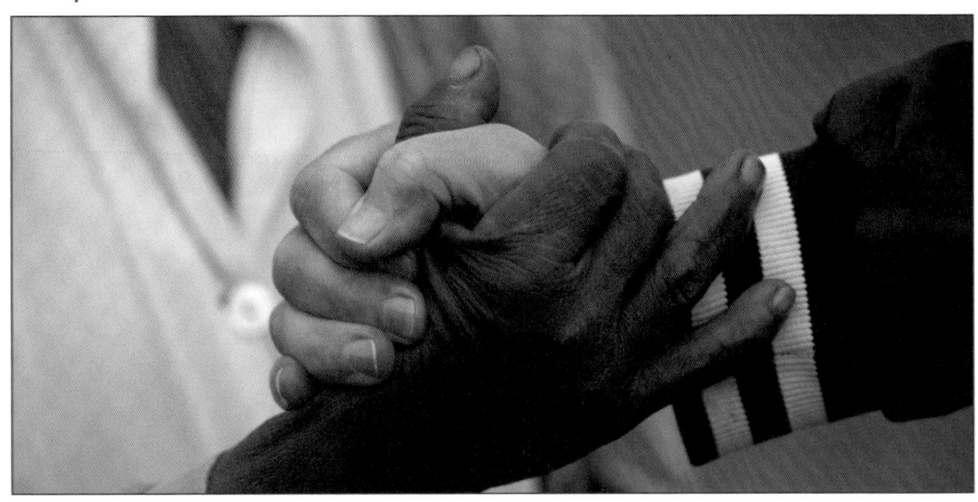

the truth commission's offer of amnesty, more than seven thousand people applied for amnesty and testified, often shamefacedly, in public.

Although the truth commission had many critics—some who heard how brutally their loved ones had died could never forgive their killers—it is generally considered a successful program that was of immense benefit in the transition to a true democracy. In the end it helped the young nation turn its eyes from the past and toward the future. Perhaps most important of all, the permanent record it created—in particular, the thousands of hours of gripping testimony on live television—forced the world, not just South Africans, to recognize that apartheid was an inherently evil system whose lessons must not be ignored.

Notes

Introduction: A Triumph of the Human Spirit

1. Quoted in Mark Mathabane, *Kaffir Boy*. New York: Macmillan, 1986, p. 93.
2. Quoted in Peter Ackerman and Jack Duvall, *A Force More Powerful*. New York: St. Martin's, 2000, p. 337.
3. Quoted in Ackerman and Duvall, *Force More Powerful*, p. 368.

Chapter One: The Roots of Apartheid

4. David Mason, *A Traveller's History of South Africa*. New York: Interlink, 2004, p. 79.
5. Quoted in Mason, *Traveller's History of South Africa*, p. 81.
6. Brian Lapping, *Apartheid: A History*. New York: George Braziller, 1987, p. 19.
7. Frank Welsh, *South Africa: A Narrative History*. New York: Kodansha International, 1999, p. 334.
8. Lapping, *Apartheid*, p. 54.
9. Quoted in Lapping, *Apartheid*, p. 41.

Chapter Two: A "Diabolical" Plan

10. Quoted in Mason, *Traveller's History of South Africa*, p. 191.
11. Quoted in Roger B. Beck, *The History of South Africa*. Westport, CT: Greenwood Press, 2000, p. 124.
12. Quoted in Anthony Sampson, *Mandela: The Authorized Biography*. New York: Knopf, 1999.
13. Beck, *History of South Africa*, p. 126.
14. Quoted in Welsh, *South Africa*, p. 417.
15. Quoted in David Mermelstein, ed., *The Anti-Apartheid Reader*. New York: Grove Press, 1987, p. 95.
16. Quoted in Welsh, *South Africa*, p. 430.
17. Quoted in Beck, *History of South Africa*, p. 127.
18. Quoted in Leonard Thompson, *A History of South Africa*. New Haven, CT: Yale University Press, 1990, p. 194.
19. Welsh, *South Africa*, p. 416.
20. Quoted in Mason, *Traveller's History of South Africa*, p. 198.

Chapter Three: Resistance and Repression

21. Dougie Oakes, ed., *Illustrated History of South Africa: The Real Story*. Pleasantville, NY: Reader's Digest, 1989, p. 491.
22. Nancy L. Clark and William H. Worger, *South Africa: The Rise and Fall of Apartheid*. London: Pearson Longman, 2004, p. 55.
23. Quoted in Sampson, *Mandela*, p. 75.
24. Nelson Mandela, "No Easy Walk to Freedom," presidential address by Nelson Mandela to the ANC (Transvaal) Congress, September 21, 1953.

ANC Today: Online Voice of the African National Congress. www.anc.org.za/.
25. *ANC Today: Online Voice of the African National Congress,* "The Freedom Charter Adopted at the Congress of the People, Kliptown, on 26 June 1955." www.anc.org.za/.
26. Quoted in Martin Meredith, *Nelson Mandela: A Biography.* New York: St. Martin's Press, 1997, p. 182.
27. Sampson, *Mandela,* p. 107.

Chapter Four: Grand Apartheid

28. Quoted in Oakes, *Illustrated History of South Africa,* p. 378.
29. Sebastian Mallaby, *After Apartheid: The Future of South Africa.* New York: Times Books, 1992, p. 136.
30. Quoted in Sampson, *Mandela,* p. 127.
31. Quoted in Lapping, *Apartheid,* p. 136.
32. Quoted in Ackerman and Duvall, *Force More Powerful,* p. 340.
33. Nelson Mandela, *The Struggle Is My Life.* New York: Pathfinder, 1986, pp. 122–23.
34. Quoted in Meredith, *Nelson Mandela,* pp. 262–63.
35. Quoted in Jonathan Paton, *The Land and People of South Africa.* New York: J.B. Lippincott, 1990, pp. 206–207.
36. Quoted in Meredith, *Nelson Mandela,* p. 272.

Chapter Five: Black Consciousness and the Soweto Uprising

37. Clark and Worger, *South Africa,* p. 76.
38. Stephen Biko, *I Write What I Like.* London: Bowerdean Press, 1996, p. 49.
39. Quoted in Robert M. Price, *The Apartheid State in Crisis.* New York: Oxford University Press, 1991, p. 52.
40. Biko, *I Write What I Like,* p. 100.
41. Beck, *History of South Africa,* p. 160.
42. Quoted in Clark and Worger, *South Africa,* p. 76.
43. Quoted in Mason, *Traveller's History of South Africa,* p. 225.
44. Quoted in Beck, *History of South Africa,* p. 162.
45. Quoted in Mason, *Traveller's History of South Africa,* p. 227.
46. Quoted in Lapping, *Apartheid,* p. 162.

Chapter Six: Battling the "Great Crocodile"

47. Quoted in Nelson Mandela, *Long Walk to Freedom.* New York: Little, Brown, 1994, p. 478.
48. Quoted in Welsh, *South Africa,* p. 479.
49. Quoted in Mason, *Traveller's History of South Africa,* p. 230.
50. Beck, *History of South Africa,* p. 162.
51. Ackerman and Duvall, *Force More Powerful,* p. 347.
52. Ackerman and Duvall, *Force More Powerful,* p. 348.
53. Quoted in Welsh, *South Africa,* p. 485.
54. Quoted in Clark and Worger, *South Africa,* p. 90.
55. Quoted in Beck, *History of South Africa,* p. 172.
56. Nelson Mandela, "Statement Delivered by Zinzi Mandela to Mass Meeting, Jabulani Stadium," February 10, 1985. *ANC Today: Online Voice of the African National Congress.* www.anc.org.za/.
57. Quoted in Lapping, *Apartheid,* p. 178.

Chapter Seven: The End of Apartheid

58. Quoted in Welsh, *South Africa,* pp. 501–02.
59. Quoted in Ackerman and Duvall, *Force More Powerful,* p. 363.
60. Ackerman and Duvall, *Force More Powerful,* p. 366.
61. Quoted in Clark and Worger, *South Africa,* p. 147.
62. Beck, *History of South Africa,* p. 181.
63. Nelson Mandela, "Nelson Mandela's Address to Rally in Cape Town on His Release from Prison," February 11, 1990. *ANC Today: Online Voice of the African National Congress.* www.anc.org.za/.
64. Mandela, "Nelson Mandela's Address to Rally in Cape Town."
65. Quoted in Clark and Worger, *South Africa,* p. 104
66. Mandela, *Long Walk to Freedom,* p. 526.
67. Welsh, *South Africa,* p. 508.
68. Meredith, *Nelson Mandela,* pp. 516–17.
69. Meredith, *Nelson Mandela,* p. 518.
70. F.W. de Klerk, speech to the nation, May 2, 1994. www.fwdklerk.org.za/download_archive/94_02_05_Election_Results_A.doc.
71. Nelson Mandela, "Statement of the President of the African National Congress, Nelson Mandela, at His Inauguration as President of the Democratic Republic of South Africa," May 10, 1994. *ANC Today: Online Voice of the African National Congress.* www.anc.org.za/.
72. Mandela, "Statement of the President of the African National Congress."

Epilogue: Truth and Reconciliation

73. Nelson Mandela, "Nelson Mandela's 100 Day Speech to Parliament," August 18, 1994. University of Pennsylvania, African Studies Center. www.africa.upenn.edu.

For Further Information

Books

Nancy L. Clark and Wlliam H. Worger, *South Africa: The Rise and Fall of Apartheid.* London: Pearson Longman, 2004. A useful, concise study of apartheid. The chapter on the collapse of apartheid is especially informative.

Jillian Edelstein, *Truth and Lies.* New York: New Press, 2002. Testimony presented before the Truth and Reconciliation Commission is combined with photographs to produce a strong indictment of apartheid.

David Goodman, *Fault Lines: Journeys into the New South Africa.* Berkeley: University of California Press, 1999. Profiles of eight South Africans on all sides of the apartheid issue, including a man who tortured and killed for the NP government.

Nadine Gordimer and David Goldblatt, *Lifetimes Under Apartheid.* New York: Knopf, 1986. A Nobel Prize–winning author supplies commentary to accompany stark, powerful photographs documenting the harshness of living under apartheid.

Antjie Krog, *Country of My Skull.* New York: Random House, 2000. A harrowing account of the work of the Truth and Reconciliation Commission by a South African poet.

Brian Lapping, *Apartheid: A History.* New York: George Braziller, 1987. Although written before the fall of apartheid, this is an excellent portrayal of the origins and development of an all-powerful racist state.

Sebastian Mallaby, *After Apartheid: The Future of South Africa.* New York: Times Books, 1992. An exceptionally readable and balanced analysis of how apartheid came into being and why it could not last.

Nelson Mandela, *Mandela: An Illustrated Autobiography.* Boston: Little, Brown, 1994. An abridged version of Mandela's *Long Walk to Freedom,* this accessible, illustrated autobiography of apartheid's most famous opponent is highly recommended for young readers.

Mark Mathabane, *Kaffir Boy.* New York: Macmillan, 1986. A vivid memoir by a black South African writer who describes growing up under apartheid and his improbable escape from the system.

Tim McKee, *No More Strangers Now: Young Voices from a New South Africa.* New York: Dorling Kindersley, 1998.

Twelve young South Africans, describing what it was like to grow up under apartheid, offer hope for the future.

Jonathan Paton, *The Land and People of South Africa.* New York: J.B. Lippincott, 1990. South African history through the fall of apartheid. Large print and illustrations make this book a good source for young readers.

Anthony Sampson, *Mandela: The Authorized Biography.* New York: Knopf, 1999. Highly recommended, thorough account of Mandela's remarkable life.

Web Sites

ANC Today: Online Voice of the African National Congress (www.anc.org.za/index.html). This ANC site maintains an archive of all of Nelson Mandela's speeches, as well as many other historical documents related to apartheid.

Apartheid Museum (www.apartheidmuseum.org). An online site connected to a museum in Johannesburg dedicated to telling the story of apartheid.

Human Rights: Historical Images of Apartheid in South Africa (www.un.org/av/photo/subjects/apartheid.htm). A photographic archive, sponsored by the United Nations, that offers a vivid record of apartheid that is a useful companion to documents and speeches.

Index

Picture Credits

Cover: © Peter Turnley/CORBIS

AP/Wide World Photo, 13, 39, 51, 56, 59, 86

© Bettmann/CORBIS, 10 (lower right), 25, 32, 35, 48,61

© E.O. Hoppe/CORBIS, 23

© Hulton-Deutsch Collection/CORBIS, 49

© Gideon Mendel/CORBIS, 89

© Charles O'Rear/CORBIS, 53

© Reuters/CORBIS, 82

© Stapleton Collection/CORBIS, 19

© David Turnley/CORBIS, 31, 66, 84, 90

© Peter Turnley/CORBIS, 10(lower right), 11(lower right), 79

AFP/Getty Images, 76

Hulton Archive by Getty Images, 10(upper left), 18, 27(lower), 60

Time-Life Pictures/Getty Images, 27(upper), 38, 42, 47, 70, 71

Library of Congress, 10(upper right,lower left), 11(upper right)

About the Author

A former editor at *Reminisce* magazine, Michael J. Martin is a freelance writer whose home overlooks the Mississippi River in Lansing, Iowa. He has written more than a dozen books for young people, as well as magazine articles for publications like *Boys' Life and Timeline,* and has a master's degree in educational psychology from the University of Wisconsin–Milwaukee. His most recent books for Lucent are a biography of test pilot Chuck Yeager, *The Korean War: Life as a POW,* and *Teen Depression.*